kid chef bakes

kid chef BAKES

The KIDS COOKBOOK FOR ASPIRING BAKERS

Lisa Huff

ROCKRIDGE PRESS

For general information on our other products and services or to obtain technical support, please contact our Customer Care Department within the U.S. at (866) 744-2665, or outside the U.S. at (510) 253-0500.

Rockridge Press publishes its books in a variety of electronic and print formats. Some content that appears in print may not be available in electronic books, and vice versa.

All photography © Hélène Dujardin/Food styling by Tami Hardeman/prop styling by Angela Hall except pages 34, 72 & 83: © Jennifer Davick; pages 67, 77, 79, 93, 117, 125, 135, 145, 151, 163, 173, 177 & 187: © Lisa Huff; page 133: Ellie Baygulov/Stocksy. Illustrations: TongSur/iStock, pages 11-13.
Author photo © Andrea Topalian

ISBN: Print 978-1-62315-942-9 | eBook 978-1-62315-943-6

Contents

Foreword

Despite major advancements in how we treat cardiovascular disease, it remains the number one killer of men and women in the United States and across much of the world. Unfortunately, too many of our health care dollars are spent on treating the sick, rather than on prevention. In recent years, however, the focus has shifted to ways we can prevent and even potentially reverse cardiovascular disease. These new strategies are largely what drove me to focus on preventive cardiology.

At the core of preventing cardiovascular disease is a heart-healthy diet. As the daughter of Greek immigrant parents, I grew up eating a balanced Mediterranean diet, with all of the essential nutrients. But early in my medical training I tried to convince my family that a typical low-fat diet was better for cardiovascular health because that is what research showed at the time. I became so focused on limiting fat, I found myself failing to include heart-healthy nutrients in my own diet.

Fortunately, I have since learned to appreciate the value of a "good fat" diet, as opposed to a "low-fat" diet. The medical community has also embraced this principle, realizing that promoting a low-fat diet without also emphasizing good nutrition may have actually *contributed* to a rise in obesity and diabetes—both closely linked to cardiovascular disease.

Although the medical community endorses several diets (the American Heart Association diet, the DASH or Dietary Approaches to Stop Hypertension diet, the Mediterranean diet, and various versions of a whole food plant-based diet), they all have something in common: a strong preference for fruits, vegetables, seeds, nuts, legumes, and whole grains.

In medicine, we rely on data to choose the best possible care for our patients. The most useful data comes from trials in which patients are randomly given one kind of treatment or another and observed over time. The results of these trials have shown a clear connection between diet and disease. Although all of the diets I've mentioned have benefits, the best evidence we have to date is for the Mediterranean diet.

Several trials have examined the effects of the Mediterranean diet on heart attack survivors, and all have shown that patients stay healthier and live longer when they follow the diet. In 2012, a large-scale trial in Spain also showed the tremendous benefits of the Mediterranean diet in people who had not yet developed heart disease, reducing the incidence of heart attack and stroke.

The benefits of the Mediterranean diet include reduced blood pressure, improved cholesterol levels, and better blood sugar regulation—all cardiac risk factors. The nutrients in the diet also appear to have protective effects on the heart; by reducing inflammation and improving the responsiveness of arteries, they likely contribute to a separate mechanism of heart disease reduction.

When scoring various populations to see how close their typical diet comes to an ideal Mediterranean diet, research has shown that the higher the score, the lower the risk for cardiovascular disease and cancer, and the longer the life span. The diet has also been shown to be effective for weight loss and weight maintenance. It has a high rate of compliance, possibly because eating good fats and plenty of fiber leaves people feeling full and satisfied.

As Dorothy Calimeris describes so beautifully in the introduction to this book, the Mediterranean diet is not just about foods, but also about a lifestyle that has proven to be beneficial in reducing disease. That lifestyle includes regular physical activity, a sense of community, and reduced stress. We know that each of these principles is related to better health and is a major focus of preventive care.

Finding simple ways to incorporate the Mediterranean diet and lifestyle into our lives could have a major impact on our health and happiness. In this book, Dorothy puts forward a delicious assortment of Mediterranean dishes with a focus on those nutrients believed to be most essential, along with limited amounts of meats, sweets, and refined grains. The recipes are simple and doable—even for people like me with busy schedules. I commend her for this tremendous work, which will undoubtedly make my work as a cardiologist easier!

—EUGENIA GIANOS, MD

ABOUT THE FOREWORD CONTRIBUTOR

EUGENIA GIANOS, MD, is an assistant professor of medicine at the NYU School of Medicine and director of the Preventive Cardiology Fellowship program. She directs a unique course on dietary strategies for cardiovascular risk reduction, serving to educate clinicians about this important area of cardiovascular prevention. An active member of the American Heart Association, the American College of Cardiology and the National Lipid Association, she was named a *Super Doctors* Rising Star by the *New York Times Magazine* in 2013 and 2014.

Introduction

I grew up in a household that was eating a Mediterranean diet before we knew it was called that. Since we were a Greek-American family, we ate Greek food. My grandparents had a farm in the San Joaquin Valley in California, so we had fresh produce regularly, and my uncle cured and pressed his own olive oil. Almost every weekend involved tables laden with dishes of olives, feta cheese, sliced tomatoes and cucumbers, boiled greens, yogurt, roasted meats, and fresh fruit. I didn't understand how good I had it.

As I developed as a chef, I was fascinated by all types of cuisines and spent many years cooking everything *but* Mediterranean foods! After I exhausted my culinary tour of the world, though, I felt myself being pulled back to my roots. The food of my childhood is simple, easy to prepare, vibrant, delicious, and feels good in my body. In fact, I credit the healthy foods of the Mediterranean diet for my overall good health.

With so many diets being talked about in the media these days, it's hard to determine the best way to eat. The Mediterranean diet is a simple plan that relies heavily on plants, focusing on seasonal fruits and vegetables, whole grains, legumes, nuts, and olive oil. Seafood, poultry, meats, eggs, and yogurt are all on the menu, but not as the main attraction. You can enjoy sweets, but primarily in the form of fresh fruit–with the occasional pastry or dessert to be thoroughly enjoyed with a good cup of coffee. And chocolate! Yes, chocolate! Spain and France are noted for their rich, thick hot chocolate and velvety smooth dark chocolate bars, and this too is part of healthy eating.

This is a diet and lifestyle of abundance. It's about the excitement of seeing the first asparagus and strawberries of spring, the aroma and vivid colors of summer melons. And let's not forget tomatoes–a riot of colors and varieties in late summer and early fall. It's shopping with your eyes, looking at what is fresh and beautiful, enjoying the best nature

has to offer. It's also about taking the time to shop, to cook, to eat, to visit, to decompress. Even with our high-octane busy lives, there are small things we can do daily to de-stress: Promote digestion with a 10-minute walk after dinner; take your lunch break outside and eat on a bench in the sun; eat breakfast without the news on in the background. These are all ways to combat stress and eat mindfully.

In this book you will find some great tools to help you embrace the traditional Mediterranean diet while living the good life.

- All the recipes focus on the core Mediterranean diet principles of eating whole grains, vegetables and fruits, legumes, nuts, olive oil, cheese and yogurt, fish, poultry, eggs, wine, and lean meat.

- Easy, simple recipes use affordable ingredients that you can find without much effort.

- Many of the recipes can be made ahead, frozen, and reheated.

- I've included tips for modifying the recipes to include allergen-friendly options.

- There's advice on buying and storing ingredients such as organic produce, olive oil, low-mercury seafood, sustainable poultry and eggs, and meats.

- You'll find practical tips for incorporating the Mediterranean diet's low-stress lifestyle into your own busy life.

one

Savoring the Good Life

La dolce vita: **The sweet life.** The Italian phrase captures the essence of the Mediterranean diet traditionally eaten in Italy and Greece. At the heart of this philosophy are the enjoyment of family, friends, and food. The fertile land and mild climate produce an abundance of luscious fruits and vegetables, the pastures and farmyards yield the finest livestock, and the warm sea teems with delectable seafood. In markets, wineries, bakeries, and kitchens, the gifts of nature are transformed into simply delicious food and drink.

Around the dining room table, and in trattorias, tavernas, and cafés, people gather to share meals that can last for hours. Parents and children, cousins and grandparents, sit down to plates of roasted vegetables and hearty bread, bowls of bean soup and chilled fruit, and bottles of emerald-green olive oil and ruby-red wine. The food is flavorful, varied, and abundant, but laughter, gossip, and confidences are the main courses. After dinner comes a stroll, to take in the air and wind down from the day. This is the Mediterranean diet, one of the healthiest on Earth.

A Healthy Diet Rooted in Tradition

Since as far back as the Bronze Age (about 3300 to 1200 BCE), when people living around the Mediterranean Sea turned from hunting and gathering to farming, Mediterranean cultures have relied on plant foods as their primary source of nutrition. Known as the Cradle of Civilization, the Mediterranean Basin–southern Europe, the Middle East, and North Africa–has seen the rise and fall of mighty cultures, all of which sustained themselves with the Mediterranean diet in various forms. Ancient Egyptians, Assyrians, Persians, Greeks, and Romans spun broadly diverse cuisines out of the same basic ingredients: olive oil, grain, vegetables, fruit, and smaller amounts of dairy products, seafood, meat, and red wine.

At its height in the 2nd century CE, the Roman Empire covered the entire Mediterranean Basin, stretched north to Germany and Britain, and east to Iraq and Iran. Exotic flavors and new culinary methods filtered into the Mediterranean mix. After Europeans reached the Americas in the 15th century, explorers brought back even more "new" foods, such as tomatoes, peppers, corn, potatoes, and new varieties of beans. By the 19th century, the food of impoverished, rural southern Italy and Greece looked a lot like the Mediterranean diet does today.

Until the last few decades of the 20th century, wealthier European and North American countries took little interest in that "peasant" cuisine. But after World War II, scientists noticed that Greece and southern Italy had the highest concentration of centenarians in the world. Even though the locals ate a "poor person's" diet, they had among the world's lowest rates of heart disease and certain cancers. Meanwhile, those diseases were rampant in prosperous America.

To find out why, University of Minnesota physiologist Ancel Keys launched the Seven Countries Study in 1958. It tracked the health of nearly 13,000 men ages 40 to 59 in Finland, Italy, Greece, Japan, the Netherlands, the United States, and Yugoslavia. The researchers found that the men of the Greek island of Crete were the healthiest in the world–90 percent less likely to die from a heart attack than American men. In 1975, Ancel and Margaret Keys described the Mediterranean Diet in their book *How to Eat Well and Stay Well the Mediterranean Way*. The Seven Countries Study continues to follow its remaining original participants, to show the benefits of the Mediterranean diet well into old age.

Hundreds of other studies have confirmed the benefits of the Mediterranean diet. A study that began in 1986 (and was published in 2013) of 10,670 American women in their late 50s and early 60s found that those who ate a Mediterranean-style diet were about 40 percent more likely to stay healthy past age 70. In 1993, the Harvard School of Public Health, the World Health Organization, and Oldways Preservation Trust, an organization dedicated to raising awareness of traditional

LONGEVITY IN THE BLUE ZONES

Why do certain people live such long lives? In 2004, the National Geographic Society investigated that question by visiting regions whose people are known for their longevity. The researchers found five places where people reach the age of 100 ten times more often than in most of the United States. These so-called Blue Zones—Ikaria in Greece, Nicoya in Costa Rica, Okinawa in Japan, Sardinia in Italy, and Loma Linda, California's Seventh-Day Adventist community—shared some key diet and lifestyle features.

One of these features was insulation from outside influences that might change the status quo. The geography and history of the two Mediterranean Blue Zones (the islands of Sardinia and Ikaria) have isolated them from

outsiders. They have been able to preserve their traditional, healthy cultures. Sardinians have an extra advantage too: They actually carry a longevity gene. You probably don't have those advantages, but you can adopt the healthy eating habits and active, social lifestyle that play an even bigger role in Sardinian and Ikarian longevity.

The people of Ikaria and Sardinia eat a Mediterranean diet, putting legumes (beans) front and center and eating meat no more than five times per month. They drink goat's and sheep's milk, which are more nutritious and easier to digest than cow's milk. Antioxidant-rich herbal teas and red wine are favorite beverages. The islanders customarily stop eating when they're 80 percent full, and many fast occasionally, eating about 30 percent fewer calories than normal.

Life moves slowly on Ikaria and Sardinia, keeping stress to a minimum. Residents often take midafternoon naps, and they get plenty of outdoor exercise. The fine climate and hilly landscape, as well as tradition, encourage physical activity, both at work (gardening, chores, farming, fishing) or leisure (strolling to the market, visiting friends). Family and friends are a priority. Many residents live in extended families, in which generations value and care for one another. In these small island communities, people know their neighbors and maintain close, lifelong ties to their friends. And every day, they laugh together.

foods, developed the Mediterranean diet that's popular today, and designed the Mediterranean Diet Food Pyramid (see page 18). In 2015, the US Department of Health and Human Services published its version of the diet.

The Mediterranean Tradition

The Mediterranean Diet is based on principles that reflect the Mediterranean's historical eating and lifestyle patterns, as well as modern scientific analysis of the traditions of the Mediterranean region. The basic principles are simple and inviting.

Eat and drink in moderation. The traditional Mediterranean diet is one of balance and moderation, not excess or self-denial. You'll enjoy your food more and feel better if you eat only until your hunger is satisfied, not until you're stuffed. If you drink wine or other alcoholic beverages, don't overdo it: You'll have a clearer head today and avoid a hangover tomorrow.

Eat fresh, seasonal, locally grown, and, ideally, organic foods. Throughout the Mediterranean, most foods are still farmed cleanly and naturally, in virtually the same way they have been for generations. Food raised this way really does taste better, and it's generally more nutritious than commercially produced food.

Eliminate processed foods. One reason the people from Mediterranean regions have been and continue to be healthier than

Americans is that they eat almost entirely natural, unprocessed food. Since the 1950s, the "modern" American diet has incorporated more and more fast food, microwave meals, and prepackaged convenience foods that tend to be high in sodium, saturated fat, and sugar. None of those things contribute anything positive to your health.

Center your diet around plant-based foods, and vary your choices. This means fresh fruits and vegetables, legumes, whole grains, and nuts and seeds. Combine foods of different colors and textures to get the nutrients you need. Vegetables are also high in fiber and make you feel full longer, so you don't get hungry as often.

Replace unhealthy fats with healthy fats. Olive oil, arguably the most important ingredient in Mediterranean cooking, is the king of good fats. This delicious, nutritious, monounsaturated oil should be your main source of fat. Why? It's a monounsaturated fat, a type of fat that can help reduce the level of bad cholesterol (LDL) in your blood, which can reduce your risk of heart disease and stroke. Other monounsaturated oils, such as canola, peanut, and sesame oils, are healthy too. You can easily use healthy fats to replace unhealthy saturated animal fats, such as butter and lard, and trans fats such as margarine and partially hydrogenated vegetable oils. These kinds of fats raise your LDL levels and your risk of heart disease.

Eat small to moderate amounts of seafood and poultry. Animal protein plays a supporting rather than a starring role in traditional

Mediterranean meals, and sometimes doesn't appear at all. Fish and shellfish show up most frequently, and should be your first protein choices. They're full of vitamins and healthy fats; cold-water fish are especially abundant in beneficial omega-3 fats, which can lower your blood triglyceride level (an indicator of heart health) and reduce your risk of dying from a heart attack or stroke by as much as 50 percent. Poultry is high in protein and low in fat. Eggs are another nutritious choice.

Eat a little dairy each day. Unlike the typical American diet, the traditional Mediterranean diet isn't overloaded with dairy. Though it's a significant source of calcium, which is so important to bone health, dairy can be high in saturated fat. Enjoy lower-fat cheeses in small amounts. Choose low-fat and nonfat plain yogurt and milk.

Reduce your red meat intake to a few times per month, and stick to leaner cuts. Traditionally, Mediterranean peoples ate red meat perhaps once per month, or on special occasions. Meat was most often eaten in small amounts, often just as a flavoring in sauces or vegetable dishes. You don't have to cut back quite that much; just eat smaller portions less often.

Limit sugary treats. Fresh fruit is the most common dessert in the Mediterranean, while more decadent sweets are eaten only occasionally. Cutting back on cakes, cookies, ice cream, candy, and sweetened beverages such as soda will keep you healthier and make your sweets a true treat.

Drink a glass of wine with your meals. Wine has always been part of Mediterranean meals, and as it turns out, red wine in particular has health benefits–such as lowering your risk of heart attack and heart disease, stroke, and diabetes–when consumed in moderate amounts. You don't have to drink alcohol, but if you do, limit yourself to one five-ounce glass daily if you're a woman or two five-ounce glasses if you're a man.

Enjoy relaxing meals. Meals in the Mediterranean are as much about good company as they are about good food. As often as you can–at least a couple of times per week–share a leisurely meal with your family and friends. Even when you're alone, step away from your desk or out of your car, sit down at the table or on a park bench, and turn off the TV, phone, and computer. Take your time and savor every bite.

Engage in regular physical activity. Until the late 20th century, most people did a significant amount of physical work. One byproduct of all that exercise was good health. Even today, people in Mediterranean countries choose to walk rather than drive when they can, and usually take a stroll after dinner. Add moderate exercise to your routine to keep your body and mind healthy.

WHAT TO EAT
on the Mediterranean Diet

Whenever you start a new diet, there's a tendency to focus on what you can't eat. But it's so much more enjoyable to think about what you can eat—especially on this diet, which offers so many delicious choices. What foods, exactly, fit into the Mediterranean diet? Each of your three main daily meals should contain whole grains, fresh nonstarchy vegetables, and fresh fruit. Daily or weekly, add a few servings of starchy vegetables, legumes, healthy fats, seafood, poultry, eggs, dairy products, and, if you like, a little red wine. Every so often, treat yourself to some red meat or a decadent sweet.

Typical Foods of the Mediterranean Diet

FRUITS & VEGETABLES

Green & leafy vegetables Arugula, bok choy, broccoli, broccoli rabe, collard greens, kale, lettuce (not iceberg), mustard greens, spinach, Swiss chard

Red & orange vegetables Bell peppers (orange, red, yellow), carrots, tomatoes

Starchy vegetables Corn, fresh peas, potatoes, sweet potatoes, winter squash (acorn, butternut, pumpkin, etc.)

Other vegetables Artichokes, asparagus, beets, bell peppers (green), Brussels sprouts, cabbage, cauliflower, celery, cucumbers, eggplant, garlic, green beans, mushrooms, onions, radishes, turnips, wax beans, yellow squash, zucchini
➥ *Fresh is best, but frozen will do; avoid canned vegetables, which have added salt.*

Fruit Apples, apricots, bananas, berries, cherries, citrus fruits, dates, figs, grapes, kiwis, mangoes, melons, nectarines, peaches, pears, pineapple, plums, pomegranates
➥ *Fruits canned in their own juice or frozen without added sugar are pretty good alternatives.*

GRAINS & LEGUMES

Whole grains Barley, buckwheat, bulgur wheat, oats, quinoa, rice (brown or wild), whole-grain bread, whole-grain cereal, whole-grain cornmeal (flour, grits, polenta), whole-wheat flour, crackers, and pasta
➥ *Many whole-grain breads and pastas also contain refined grain; read the labels.*

Legumes Dry or canned beans (including black-eyed peas, chickpeas, etc.), fresh lima, fava, lentils, soybeans (edamame), split peas, tofu
➥ *Canned beans are fine if they're rinsed before eating; try to find low-sodium.*

NUTS, SEEDS & OILS

Nuts Almonds, cashews, peanuts, pine nuts (pignoli), walnuts, nut butters
➥ *Unsalted and raw varieties are the healthiest.*

Seeds Chia, flax, pumpkin (pepitas), poppy, sesame, sunflower, tahini

Oils & fruit Avocado, canola, extra-virgin olive, grapeseed, peanut, sesame, walnut oil and avocados and olives

HERBS, SPICES & FLAVORINGS

Herbs Basil, chives, cilantro, dill, mint, oregano, parsley, rosemary, sage, tarragon, thyme

Spices Black pepper, cayenne pepper, chile powder, cinnamon, cloves, coriander, cumin, curry, ginger powder, mustard powder, nutmeg, paprika
➥ *Unlimited, except salt*

Flavorings Unsweetened cocoa powder, honey, hot sauce, pure maple syrup, low-sodium soy sauce, vanilla extract, vinegars

SEAFOOD

Fish Catfish, cod, herring, mackerel, pollock, salmon, sardines, tilapia, trout, tuna
➥ *Canned fish without added salt is fine, packed either in water or olive oil; there is no such thing as organic seafood.*

Shellfish Clams, crabs, crawfish, lobsters, mussels, octopus, oysters, scallops, shrimp, squid

DAIRY

Dairy products Plain nonfat or low-fat yogurt, skim or 2 percent milk, and naturally low-fat cheeses (such as Camembert, cottage, farmers, feta, goat, haloumi, mozzarella, Neufchatel, Parmesan, ricotta, and part-skim Edam)

Eggs Chicken, duck, quail

MEAT & POULTRY

Red meat Beef (flank, sirloin, eye or top round, tenderloin, top loin, rump roast, extra-lean hamburger), bison, lamb (loin chops, leg, shank), pork (center loin, tenderloin), venison
➥ *Choose the leanest cuts.*

Poultry Chicken, Cornish hen, duck, goose, quail, turkey
➥ *Breast meat is lowest in fat, followed by thigh and wing meat.*

ALCOHOL & SWEETS

Alcohol Red wine
➥ *Pinot noir is lower in alcohol than other red wines, even the dry ones.*

Sweets Dark chocolate, dried fruit
➥ *Sweeten desserts with fruit purées and juices.*

The Mediterranean Diet Pyramid

Introduced in 1993, the Mediterranean Diet Pyramid was developed by the Harvard School of Public Health, the World Health Organization, and Oldways. The bottom of the pyramid shows the plant-based foods that are the foundation of a healthy Mediterranean diet. Above that are progressively narrower tiers that show the other food groups in the diet: The higher up in the pyramid, the smaller the amounts of those foods you should eat. At the apex are foods you should only eat occasionally, if at all. The water and wine glasses beside the pyramid show that they're an important part of the diet, while the box supporting the pyramid shows key elements of the Mediterranean lifestyle.

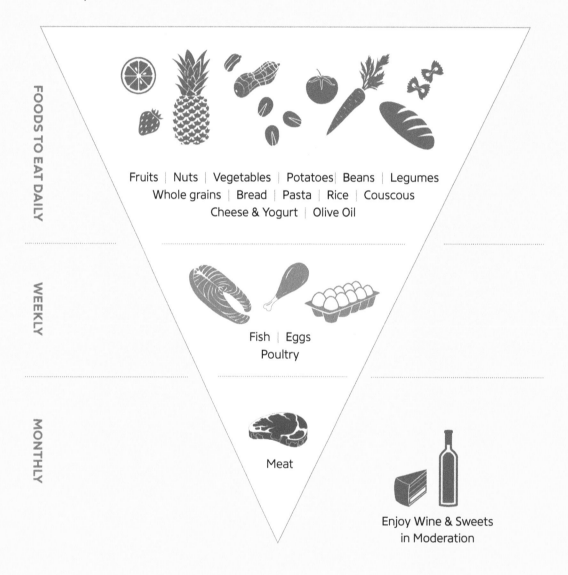

FOODS TO EAT DAILY

Fruits | Nuts | Vegetables | Potatoes | Beans | Legumes
Whole grains | Bread | Pasta | Rice | Couscous
Cheese & Yogurt | Olive Oil

WEEKLY

Fish | Eggs
Poultry

MONTHLY

Meat

Enjoy Wine & Sweets
in Moderation

HOW MUCH TO EAT
on the Mediterranean Diet

Moderation is the watchword of the Mediterranean diet. No matter the food, the more you eat, the more calories you take in. Portion control guarantees you get the nutrition you need without eating too many calories. The typical Mediterranean diet includes about 2,000 calories per day. You may need to adjust that a bit, depending on your age, gender, and lifestyle. The lists below show you what 2,000 calories per day looks like divided into food groups and servings.

Mediterranean Diet Servings

VEGETABLES
4 to 8 per day

½ cup cut-up raw or cooked vegetables

1 cup chopped raw leafy vegetables

½ cup vegetable juice

LEGUMES
1 to 2 per day

½ cup cooked beans

¼ cup cut-up tofu

FRUITS
2 to 4 per day

½ cup cut-up fresh, frozen, or canned fruit

1 hand fruit

¼ cup dried fruit

½ cup juice

WHOLE GRAINS
4 to 6 per day

½ cup cooked grain or pasta

1 slice bread

1 (6-inch) pita

6 crackers

1 cup breakfast cereal

HERBS, SPICES & FLAVORINGS
(except salt) Unlimited

OILS AND FRUIT
4 to 6 per day

1 teaspoon olive or other healthy oil

⅛ avocado

5 olives

NUTS AND SEEDS
1 to 2 per day

12 to 15 unsalted almonds

7 to 8 walnuts or pecans

20 unsalted peanuts

2 tablespoons sunflower or sesame seeds

1 tablespoon unsalted peanut or almond butter

DAIRY PRODUCTS

1 to 3 per day

1 cup skim or low-fat milk

1 cup nonfat or low-fat plain yogurt

1 ounce naturally low-fat cheese

FISH AND SHELLFISH

less than 5 per week

1 (3-ounce) fish fillet

3 ounces shelled shellfish

POULTRY

less than 3 per week

3 ounces skinless meat

EGGS

fewer than 4 per week

1 egg

RED MEAT

less than 2 per week

3 ounces lean meat

ALCOHOL, REFINED SUGARS, SATURATED FATS

less than 10% to 13% of calories
(200 to 260 calories per day)

1 or less 5-ounce glass of wine
per day for women

2 or less 5-ounce glasses of wine
per day for men

1 (2-inch) chocolate chip cookie
(100 calories)

1 tablespoon butter
(102 calories)

1 (5-ounce) glass of wine
(125 calories)

½ cup ice cream
(137 calories)

1½ ounces dark chocolate
(216 calories)

1 slice pizza (⅛ 12-inch pie)
(231 calories)

Key Ingredients in the Mediterranean Kitchen

Good olive oil can be a bit expensive, but a little goes a long way. Fortunately, though, most of the food eaten on a Mediterranean diet is inexpensive and is easy to find. Many items are ingredients you probably have on hand in your pantry, or are easy to store, like canned beans, artichokes, and peppers. Fresh produce, seafood, meats, and poultry, on the other hand, should be eaten soon after you buy them.

The basic rule for best nutrition and sustainability practices is to buy organic and local as your first choice. If the choice is organic versus local, you can choose local over organic. Are you confused or a little overwhelmed? Don't be! I'll walk you through it all.

OLIVE OIL

Good: Extra-virgin

Better: Organic extra-virgin

Best: First-press organic extra-virgin

Olive oil is as complex in nature as any fine wine. Depending on the variety of the olive, the oil can be peppery and sharp or smooth and nutty. It can be a deep dark green or a golden green. Which oil you buy really depends on your preference, and fortunately, most purveyors of quality olive oil allow you to sample the oil before you buy. No matter what your preference, here are the core elements of purchasing a good oil.

Buy first-press extra-virgin organic if you can afford it. This ensures that you are buying the least processed olive oil. As its name implies, this is the first round of oil that is released when the olives are crushed. The next level is extra-virgin, not first press, which means it's the second press from the olives–not bad, but not as clean-tasting as first press. After that there are the designations of pure or blended, which can mean the olives have been submitted to heat (or chemicals) to extract more oil, or that the oil is combined with less expensive oils to make a blend. Avoid these oils if possible.

If you are fortunate enough to live somewhere that grows olives, by all means buy local olive oil. If not, there are excellent imported oils from Italy, Spain, Greece, and Turkey. Olive oil should be stored in a dark bottle, since exposure to light promotes spoilage. It is not necessary to refrigerate olive oil; store it in a cool dark cupboard. Stored this way, it should last at least one year. But if you follow a Mediterranean diet, you will go through it much faster than that.

PRODUCE

Good: Fresh and frozen produce, no sugars or salt added; canned beans and pickled vegetables

Better: Organic fresh and frozen vegetables, no sugars or salt added; organic canned beans and pickled vegetables

Best: Local organic vegetables, vegetables purchased from a farmers' market or received in a CSA share

If you're sometimes confused about buying fresh produce, you're not alone. It's hard to know if a melon is ripe, or how to pick an eggplant. My best advice is to ask a clerk in the produce market to help you, or buy your produce from a farmers' market. Pay attention to the choices you make and how they turn out; over time, you'll get better at picking the best tomatoes. Here are some tips for buying and storing produce.

Look for herbs that aren't wilted and are vibrant green. The best way to store herbs is to wrap the stem ends in a damp (not wet) paper towel and keep the whole thing in a sealed plastic bag in the refrigerator.

Vegetables should be firm, the skin should be smooth and unblemished, and there should be no soft or mushy spots. Soft vegetables like cucumber, zucchini, asparagus, broccoli, cauliflower, and eggplant will keep longer stored in plastic bags in the refrigerator. Hard vegetables like winter squash, pumpkins, potatoes, onions, and garlic are fine stored at room temperature, and should not be refrigerated because long chilling can change their texture.

For tomatoes, peaches, apricots, and other soft fruits, smell them. The fruit should smell like what it is. Reject fruits with no aroma, or with a fermented scent. Check the color—it should be uniform throughout the fruit without any green or brown spots. Tomatoes and stone fruits (peaches, apricots, plums, and nectarines) should be kept at room temperature and eaten when they are ripe. Refrigerating these fruits can make them mealy and will diminish their flavors. Berries should be refrigerated and are best eaten within a few days of purchasing.

Choose organic produce whenever possible. If that ends up being too expensive, take a look at Appendix A, the Dirty Dozen and the Clean Fifteen (page 216). Try to at least buy organic produce from the Dirty Dozen list, which has the most pesticide residue.

EGGS

Good: Cage-free

Better: Organic cage-free or organic pastured

Best: Certified organic, humanely raised, pastured

In the United States, eggs are not allowed to be produced with hormones or antibiotics, so if you see that on a package it's a bit of marketing copy. Free-range or cage-free may only mean that the chickens are not trapped in individual cages, but they may still be crowded into barns. So where to start?

The best way to ensure that you are buying eggs with the greatest nutritional value and flavor and the least environmental impact is to look for certified organic, humanely raised, pastured eggs. There are many criteria to be met before a product can be given that designation. If your market doesn't carry certified organic, humanely raised, pastured eggs, choose organic and cage-free.

Farmers' markets are a good place to look for high-quality eggs. Searching for them is worth the trouble too. If you don't believe me, try a side-by-side taste test, frying one conventional egg in olive oil and one high-quality egg in olive oil, and taste them. An organic, humanely raised, pastured egg will have a much more robust flavor than a conventional egg. Plus, these eggs have more vitamins and omega-3s in them than conventional eggs—how much depends on what the chickens are eating where they live.

FISH AND SEAFOOD

Good: Fresh and frozen fish

Better: Sustainably farmed fresh and frozen fish

Best: Wild and line-caught fresh and frozen fish

Fish and seafood may be the hardest to incorporate into a new diet. Many people simply don't like fish, and that's fine. You can focus on other protein sources—eggs, poultry, legumes, nuts, and the occasional red meat. However, there are lots of healthy vitamins and oils in fish, and if you want to incorporate fish into your diet, you can start slowly. Perhaps try one seafood meal per week. Begin with the less "fishy" tasting seafood like salmon, trout, tuna, crab, or shrimp, and once you're enjoying that, try some other great options like cod, halibut, scallops, tilapia, or swordfish or canned seafood like anchovies, sardines, and mussels.

Ocean fish and shellfish and river or lake fish and shellfish are all good options. When possible, buy line-caught or wild seafood, since those fish have a more complex flavor, better nutrition, and are kinder to the environment.

When buying seafood, make freshness your first priority. Fish should smell clean, not fishy, and the eyes should be clear, not cloudy. Previously frozen fish may be thawed and sold as fresh, so ask if the fish has been previously frozen. Frozen fish sold frozen is actually a better option. You can keep it in the freezer and thaw it as you need it, rather than buying something that may have been thawed for 48 hours before you buy it. When buying frozen fish read the package to see where the fish is from and if it is wild or farmed. Canned seafood is good too—sardines, anchovies, crab, oysters, tuna. The same rules apply: Read the label on the can to learn as much as you can about the fish.

Are you concerned about the mercury levels in the fish you are eating, or if the fish is sustainably caught? Mercury levels are typically highest in ocean fish, and levels of mercury vary from year to year. In the Resources section you'll find the website for the Environmental Working Group's list of the healthiest fish. You'll also find the Monterey Bay Aquarium Seafood Watch website for the most sustainable fish.

POULTRY

Good: Cage-free or free-range fresh or frozen poultry

Better: Organic cage-free or free-range fresh or frozen poultry

Best: Organic fresh or frozen air-chilled pastured poultry

The healthiest most sustainable poultry is air-chilled organic, free-range, pastured poultry. These birds are typically available at natural and specialty markets. Most chickens are processed in a water bath treated with chlorine. This rapidly cools the birds, but it uses a tremendous amount of water and exposes

HEALTHY FOOD SUBSTITUTIONS

Here's a list of healthy alternatives to foods you'll be giving up or eating a lot less of when following a Mediterranean diet.

Butter: Use olive oil (or nut oils) for baking and cooking. Some of the fat in baking recipes can be replaced with applesauce or mashed bananas. Use mashed avocado, nut butters, roasted garlic, or bean spreads as a topping on breads, vegetables, and proteins.

High-Fat Dairy: Use plain nonfat or low-fat Greek yogurt for its thick texture and high protein. Try dry hard cheeses like Parmesan; goat cheeses and feta cheese are also lower-fat alternatives.

Mayonnaise: Look for mayonnaise that is made with olive oil without sugar added. If you are unable to find it, you can make your own (page 205). Or substitute plain Greek yogurt instead.

Dairy Alternatives: The good news is a traditional Mediterranean diet doesn't include a lot of dairy, but if you can't tolerate yogurt or goat cheese feel free to substitute milk-alternative beverages and yogurts, such as those made with nuts or coconut, in these recipes. Be sure to buy plain, unflavored versions, because the flavored versions are often loaded with sugar.

Wheat alternatives: Wheat and whole grains are a part of the Mediterranean diet, but if you can't tolerate wheat or are eating gluten-free, many of the dishes made with wheat can be made with alternative grains. Those alternatives are noted in the recipes.

Sweeteners: Honey and dates are often used as sweeteners in Mediterranean recipes. You can buy granulated date and honey sugars, which are good to use in baking recipes. Even though these sweeteners have vitamins and minerals, they are still sugars and should be enjoyed only occasionally. Artificial sweeteners have no nutritional value and can increase sugar cravings and interfere with your sense of having eaten enough. They should be avoided.

the chickens to bacteria, since all chickens go through the same water. Air-chilling is a method used throughout the world, and more recently in America. The birds are still treated with chlorine but are processed through cold air, which cools them more slowly. This tenderizes them and provides better flavor, since the birds aren't soaked in water. It also decreases their exposure to bacteria and other contaminants.

Many grocery stores carry free-range birds, which are better than conventionally raised poultry. The flavor and nutritional value of free-range and pastured birds will be better than conventionally raised birds. If all else fails, at least look for birds raised without antibiotics.

RED MEAT

Good: Antibiotic-free and hormone-free fresh or frozen meats

Better: Organic antibiotic-free and hormone-free fresh or frozen meats

Best: Organic grass-fed and pastured meats

When buying meats, organic, pasture-raised and pasture-finished, or grass-fed are your best options. If pastured isn't available, look for organic and grass-fed, and if that isn't available, look for animals that are raised without antibiotics.

Grass-fed, pasture-raised, and pasture-finished means the cattle are allowed to graze the pasture up until the time of processing. You may also see designations of pasture-centered, or slaughtered at the same farm they are raised at. Grass-fed cattle may be trough-fed grasses and switched to other feed prior to

processing. When purchasing pastured meats, be sure it says "grass-fed pastured," because some ranchers still feed their cattle grains while letting them out on the pasture.

Where I live, I can find these meats at Whole Foods, which offers an animal welfare rating system. They can also be found at farmers' markets. The Resources section has information about places that sell pastured meat online.

A NOTE ABOUT WINE

The good news is wine is an integral part of the Mediterranean diet and lifestyle. And we've all heard that wine, especially red wine, is good for our heart and health. However, the recommendation here too is for moderation—one or two five-ounce glasses per day.

It's easy to get confused about which wines to buy, and to think the more expensive the wine, the better. But that's not true. There are many decent wines for under $10. Many wine shops regularly have free tastings. Find out which ones do in your area, and start attending.

If you are new to wine, it's easier to start with the lighter white wines, like chardonnay, and work your way toward the drier whites such as sauvignon blanc or pinot grigio. Once you've mastered the whites, you can transition to the reds; try a cabernet or a zinfandel.

Open wine will spoil rather quickly, so if you don't finish the bottle within one week or so of opening it, plan on using it to cook with. Store white wine in the refrigerator and red wine at room temperature away from light and heat. If you are sensitive to wine, try organic or kosher wines; they are easier to tolerate. You can also make wine spritzers by combining a half glass of wine with sparkling water and a twist of lemon.

If you don't like wine at all, or if you need to refrain from alcohol, don't worry. You will still get the heart-healthy benefits from other beverages that are loaded with antioxidants, like grape juice, pomegranate juice, and berry juice. Decaffeinated green tea or herbal tea can be a lovely way to end a meal. Or you can try some of the beverages in this book, like Chamomile Lemon Honey Iced Tea (page 41), or Cucumber Mint Smoothie (page 36).

Another option is spa water. Place slices of cucumbers and mint in a pitcher, fill with water, and chill until cold. Or add slices of lemon and thyme, or cut melon and oranges. The fruits and herbs lightly flavor the water, and the water looks beautiful and tastes delicious.

Lifestyles of the Happy and Healthy

The Mediterranean philosophy is about enjoying your food, but it also is about enjoying life and making leisure, food, family, and friends a priority–not just the food. Changing your lifestyle–even a harried, hurried, stressful one–can be hard. Here are some tips to help you on the way.

DO IT YOUR WAY

What's your personality type? Do you like to be all in, or do you approach change gradually? What would help you achieve the greatest success with this process? If you prefer slow and gradual changes, choose one or two things to change each week. You can plan to increase your vegetable consumption by one serving per day, or take a ten-minute walk after dinner. If you like to go all in, proceed to the next tips.

PLAN A COUPLE OF MENUS

Don't worry about planning a week's worth of menus. Life is unpredictable and it almost never works out the way we expect. Plan to include a few new recipes on your weekly menu, and rely on leftovers or pantry staples for one or two meals.

SHOP ONE DAY A WEEK

Before you go shopping, choose two or three recipes you want to try and make a shopping list. In addition to the ingredients you need for those recipes, do a quick inventory of all the other groceries you will need to get through the week. Do your best to limit your trips to the grocery store, to help you avoid impulse buying.

PREP FRUITS AND VEGETABLES AS YOU PUT AWAY THE GROCERIES

I leave the produce out and put everything else away. Then I prep the fruits and vegetables by cutting the berries, washing and trimming greens, tipping and tailing the beans, chopping onions, and so on. I store them in airtight containers in the fridge for easy access. It's just a week's worth–they'll keep! To make this task more enjoyable, turn on some music or listen to a podcast as you work.

SOURCING YOUR MEDITERRANEAN DIET INGREDIENTS

Most of the food grown in the Mediterranean regions is still being raised within the time-honored traditions of agriculture. It comes from family farms and ranches, or is harvested from the Mediterranean Sea by independent fishermen and seafood farmers. Chemical pesticides and fertilizers, antibiotics, and growth hormones are the exception rather than the rule. You can follow those traditions in your own Mediterranean diet by choosing certified organic and local foods.

If local or organic food isn't readily available in your area, don't worry: You'll be perfectly fine using conventionally grown ingredients.

Appendix A, "The Dirty Dozen and The Clean Fifteen" (page 216) will help you decide which produce and fruit you should buy organic, if you can, and that which is mostly pesticide-free. The most important thing is to include a lot of fresh produce into your diet.

But depending on where you live, you may be able to find organic and local produce, meat, and dairy products at your supermarket or at farmers' markets or specialty foods stores. If you can't find or afford certified organic (which adheres to government-defined limits on agricultural chemicals and food additives), go for local—fresh food produced in-season, within a couple of hundred miles of your home. It'll be tastier and more nutritious than food shipped from far away, and might be grown sustainably, without harming the environment with chemicals or ecologically harmful methods. (The term *natural*, however, can mean just about anything, so it's safe to ignore that label.)

But you won't have to worry about labels (and you can save money) if you grow your own veggies. If you have a backyard or community garden, you can farm like the Mediterraneans, using natural fertilizers and insect control—and love. These are the tastiest, and most nutritious, foods of all!

COOK AHEAD ON THE WEEKEND

Shop on Saturday and cook on Sunday, or whatever timing works best for your schedule. I like to cook the day after I shop, because then all the ingredients are in the house and waiting for me, so everything feels less stressful and more doable.

KEEP IT SIMPLE

You don't have to be slave to cooking. Do things that are easy: Roast a chicken, blanch some vegetables, make some spreads, dips, or dressings, bake one dessert, and then mix and match your pre-prepped ingredients to make different meals throughout the week.

KEEP IT INTERESTING

Commit to trying one new recipe or ingredient per week. Try things that are a stretch and take you out of your comfort zone. You may be surprised by what you like.

HAVE THE KIDS HELP

Kids love playing with food. Get the whole family involved in the planning, prepping, and cooking. It will make them more likely to taste new foods and enjoy them.

CHOOSE A RECIPE YOU LOVE, AND MAKE A LOT OF IT

Many recipes can be made in large quantities and stored in the freezer. Freeze them in individual portions for quick and easy meals. It doesn't need to be fancy—pint and quart canning jars are great for soups and sauces.

DON'T GIVE UP

You may be tempted to toss it in, especially if cooking is a challenge for you, but remember that it takes time to make lasting changes, and practice will make things easier. Don't be too hard on yourself if you find these changes hard to implement, and be kind to yourself whenever you feel guilt creep in. And if you really struggle with cooking, plan to eat several meals out, or bring them in. There are plenty of Mediterranean delis and markets where you can get premade salads, entrées, and side dishes. Pick up a roast chicken and salad greens dressed with olive oil and lemon juice for a super simple meal.

SIP A BEVERAGE AND UNWIND

Eating healthy is only one piece of the puzzle. Living well and staying relaxed—sometimes easier said than done—also contribute to a healthy lifestyle. Create a ritual of transitioning from work time to relaxation time. Sipping a hot cup of tea can be a soothing signal to destress. Another option is to have sparkling water or half a glass of wine and some vegetables, olives or a small piece of cheese when you get home. Your snack can be pre-packed in single portions to prevent you overeating before dinner.

MAKE TIME FOR MEALS

As much as possible, try to eat when you know you have time to actually sit down and eat. Dedicate time to enjoy your food. This

MEDITERRANEAN-STYLE ENTERTAINING

Mediterranean food is so delicious and popular, you will find it's a crowd-pleaser with family and friends. Here are some menu ideas.

TAPAS FROM THE GROCERY STORE

In Spain there are tapas bars that are entirely devoted to food from cans and jars. What could be easier? Here are some ideas for no-cook tapas you can get at your local supermarket. Add some wine and a crusty baguette and you're done.

From the Shelves

- Tuna packed in olive oil
- Sardines or anchovies
- Smoked mackerel or salmon
- Assorted olives (try several varieties)
- Roasted peppers
- Marinated artichoke hearts
- Canned giant white beans with garlic
- Pepperoncini
- Gherkins
- Pickled vegetables
- Toasted almonds

From the Cheese Department

- Chèvre
- Feta
- Manchego
- Parmesan (a wedge, not grated)

From the Produce Aisle

- Fresh berries, grapes, or tangerines
- Celery and carrot sticks
- Sliced cucumbers and tomatoes

OUTSIDE ON THE GRILL

Eating and cooking outside are a regular habit in the Mediterranean lifestyle, because many of the countries in that region have lovely long summers. Here's an easy menu for an outdoor party.

- Moroccan Chicken with Olives and Oranges
- Tabbouleh
- Roasted Carrots with Anise
- Arugula with Parmesan and Hazelnuts
- Yogurt Cheese with Berries

A VEGETARIAN OR VEGAN PICNIC

Another way to bring the party outside is by having a picnic. These recipes can be made ahead and travel well. Freeze the gazpacho and it can do double duty as your ice pack. Make sure you leave several hours for it to thaw before you serve it.

- Golden Gazpacho
- Roasted Vegetable and Goat Cheese Sandwich (omit the goat cheese for a vegan picnic)
- Greens and Herbs Salad
- Muesli with Apricots and Pistachios

can be gradual. If you're used to quickly grabbing meals on the go, start by dedicating 15 minutes to each meal. The next week, extend it to 20, and slowly work your way to 30 minutes. It's okay if you do this at only one meal per day.

BE MINDFUL WHEN YOU EAT

You can practice mindful eating as you practice extending your meal times. Take a moment to be grateful for the delicious food before you. Enjoy the colors and textures, inhale the aromas, and take a small bite and really feel the food in your mouth–the flavor, the texture, all the subtleties. If you're having wine, take a sip of wine with the food; how does that change it? Does it make it better or worse? Really enjoy the meal.

DINE WITH FAMILY AND FRIENDS

Community is a big part of good health. Schedule some regular time with family and friends. It can be as simple as a potluck on the last Sunday of every other month. But schedule it before life gets hectic and the fun stuff falls off the calendar.

WALK WITH FAMILY AND FRIENDS

In keeping with the Mediterranean tradition that life is better when you're with people, make part of your routine a pre- or post-meal walk. It doesn't have to be a long one; it can be around the block, as long as it gets you moving. Throughout the Mediterranean region it's very common to see entire families taking a stroll after dinner. If you live in a climate where it's too cold (or too hot) to stroll year-round, you can still gather family for weekly winter sports or just making snow angels, or even playing cards or chatting over a post-dinner cup of tea or decaf coffee.

LOOK FOR EXCUSES TO MOVE MORE

Carry things up the steps one at a time. Put the TV remote just out of reach so you have to get up to get it. Get up and get a glass of water. Set a timer on your phone or computer to remind you to get up and stretch. Park you car at the farthest end of the parking lot. Take the stairs instead of the escalator. Get rid of your cat door and get up to let the cats in and out ten times per day! Do whatever it takes to get you to move.

FIND THINGS YOU ENJOY AND MAKE TIME FOR THEM

Love the opera? Haven't been to a play in forever? Or what about the county fair? There's a reason why those good old-timey entertainments still exist: They're fun! Get a ticket and go!

GO OUTSIDE

Nothing improves a mood like a little bit of vitamin D . . . sunshine! It's easy to forget about the great outdoors, especially in the cold season. But make a point of getting at least a few minutes outside every day. If there's a park near you, take a book, sit on a bench, and read. Or walk around your neighborhood and look at the houses or gardens.

UNPLUG AND GO OLD-SCHOOL

One of the biggest stressors in our modern world is our 24/7 technological life. We never stop! I say, STOP! Create some boundaries; become unavailable. Stop checking e-mail once you're home, or at least an hour before bed. Allow yourself media breaks—it can be as simple as one hour per day or one day per week, or if you can bear it, try an entire week. You are entitled to reserve time for yourself.

MEDITATE

I bet you knew this one was coming. I know that for some people meditating is very difficult, but the health benefits are proven and substantial. Don't worry about contorting on a pillow on the floor while your mind races. Just give yourself a break from *doing* and spend a little time *being*. You can sit in a comfortable chair and listen to music for ten minutes. Listen with your whole mind by focusing your attention on the music instead of the thoughts that wander in and out of your mind. Or, sit in the chair in silence for one minute and notice the physical sensations you're experiencing. Feel the pressure of your rear end and back in the chair, and notice the textures that your fingertips feel. Note the different sounds and smells around you. Give yourself a breather and a little peace.

The Importance of Moderation

What makes a Mediterranean lifestyle so satisfying and healthy is an innate understanding of balance and moderation. People in the region definitely enjoy their food, but it's understood that food is best enjoyed when you eat just enough to satisfy your hunger but aren't stuffed. You might be served a hearty meal with large portions, but it's understood that meal is the one big meal of the day, and you'll eat light the rest of the day. And dinner is always followed by a 20- or 30-minute walk.

Until you are comfortable with what a portion size is, spend a week or two packing food in single-portion containers (refer to the chart on page 19 for portion sizes). Listen to your body's signals of hunger and fullness. Eating the traditional American diet of high fat, salt, and sugar confuses our signals for hunger and fullness. Once you start eating a healthier diet, it will be easier to know what your body needs.

two

Smoothies & Drinks

Walnut Date Smoothie

Serves 2   Prep time: 10 minutes

QUICK & EASY | VEGETARIAN | GLUTEN-FREE   Dates and walnuts are classic Mediterranean flavors, for good reason–they are delicious together. Dates are a natural sweetener; they're loaded with vitamins, minerals, and other nutrients, and are easy to digest. Walnuts are a nutritional powerhouse loaded with healthy fats, and the yogurt adds protein and probiotics, making this a fast and healthy breakfast or snack.

2 cups plain Greek yogurt
4 dates, pitted
½ cup milk
⅓ cup walnuts
½ teaspoon ground cinnamon
½ teaspoon pure vanilla extract
Ice (optional)

❀ Almonds, pistachios, and cashews all work well in this recipe. And if you like a thicker drink, add a ripe banana.

1. In a blender, combine the yogurt, dates, milk, walnuts, cinnamon, vanilla extract, and ice (if using). Blend until smooth.

2. Pour into two glasses and serve immediately.

PER SERVING Calories: 384, Protein: 21g, Total Carbohydrates: 35g, Fiber: 3g, Total Fat: 17g, Saturated Fat: 4g, Cholesterol: 20mg, Sodium: 201mg

Turmeric Carrot Smoothie

Serves 2   Prep time: 10 minutes

QUICK & EASY | VEGETARIAN | GLUTEN-FREE | BIG 8 ALLERGEN-FRIENDLY   Turmeric is a root used throughout the Far East and Middle East. It has a mild flavor and is very good for reducing inflammation. In this drink it is used in the dried powdered form, which is easy to find in the spice section of the supermarket. The sweetness of carrots just gets sweeter when combined with turmeric and the anise-like flavor of fennel. Oranges are grown throughout the Mediterranean and often enjoyed freshly squeezed. This drink is liquid sunshine.

2 cups carrot juice
1 cup freshly squeezed orange juice
½ bulb fennel
½ green apple, cored
3 tablespoons honey
½ teaspoon ground turmeric
Ice (optional)

❋ To add protein to this drink, add 1 cup Greek yogurt or ¼ cup unsalted almond butter before blending. To make it vegan, use pure maple syrup instead of honey.

1. In a blender, combine the carrot juice, orange juice, fennel, apple, honey, turmeric, and ice (if using). Blend until smooth.

2. Pour into two glasses and serve immediately.

PER SERVING Calories: 241, Protein: 3g, Total Carbohydrates: 61g, Fiber: 6g, Total Fat: 1g, Saturated Fat: 0g, Cholesterol: 0mg, Sodium: 109mg

Cucumber Mint Smoothie

Serves 2   Prep time: 15 minutes

QUICK & EASY | VEGAN | GLUTEN-FREE | BIG 8 ALLERGEN-FRIENDLY   Cucumbers and tomatoes are a cornerstone of Mediterranean salads. In this recipe they are blended into a simple, refreshing drink that is brightened by a touch of mint. I like to use sea salt in this recipe, and in general, because sea salt is less harsh-tasting than regular table salt and has more minerals since it's minimally processed. If you can't find sea salt, kosher salt is a good alternative.

1 English cucumber, peeled and cut into 1-inch pieces
1 large ripe tomato
2 tablespoons chopped fresh mint
1 tablespoon lemon juice
1 tablespoon extra-virgin olive oil
1 teaspoon sugar
¼ teaspoon sea salt
Ice (optional)

❉ This drink can easily become a cocktail by adding ½ cup Ouzo or Anisette to the blender.

1. In a blender, combine the cucumber, tomato, mint, lemon juice, olive oil, sugar, salt, and ice (if using). Blend until smooth.

2. Pour into two glasses and serve immediately.

PER SERVING Calories: 100, Protein: 2g, Total Carbohydrates: 9g, Fiber: 2g, Total Fat: 7g, Saturated Fat: 1g, Cholesterol: 0mg, Sodium: 242mg

Lassi

Serves 4   Prep time: 10 minutes

QUICK & EASY | VEGETARIAN | GLUTEN-FREE   Lassi is traditionally an Indian yogurt drink, but it uses many of the ingredients of the Mediterranean: yogurt, rosewater, and saffron. It's easy to make and can be prepared ahead of time and stored in the refrigerator. Rosewater can be found in Mediterranean markets and specialty grocery stores. Saffron can be found in the spice section of many grocery stores.

2 cups plain yogurt

1½ cups milk

½ cup sugar

2 teaspoons rosewater

A few saffron threads (optional)

1 cup ice

✲ Lassi is wonderfully versatile. If you can't find rosewater, cardamom is another traditional spice used; add 1 teaspoon ground cardamom instead. If you'd prefer a sweeter drink, use 1 cup frozen mango instead of the ice.

1. In a blender, combine the yogurt, milk, sugar, rosewater, saffron (if using), and ice. Blend until smooth.

2. Pour into four glasses and serve immediately, or store in an airtight container in the refrigerator. Shake before serving.

PER SERVING Calories: 227, Protein: 10g, Total Carbohydrates: 38g, Fiber: 0g, Total Fat: 3g, Saturated Fat: 2g, Cholesterol: 15mg, Sodium: 129mg

Almond Milk

Serves 4   Prep time: 15 minutes, plus overnight to soak

VEGAN | GLUTEN-FREE   If you haven't had homemade almond milk before, you are in for a treat. There's a freshness and delicate almond flavor that you can only taste if you make it yourself. I became frustrated trying to find a commercial almond milk that didn't have something added to it, like stabilizers, thickeners, sweeteners, and flavorings. When I make it myself, I know exactly what is in it. You will need a strainer and cheesecloth for this recipe.

2 cups raw unsalted almonds
4 cups water

❋ Almond milk can be left unflavored to use in savory dishes or for baking. For drinking, sweeten it slightly with 3 tablespoons of honey and 1 teaspoon of vanilla for the whole batch.

1. Place the almonds in a large bowl. Add enough water to cover them by 1 inch. Cover and let them sit at room temperature overnight.

2. The next day, drain the almonds and discard the water used to soak the almonds. Place the soaked almonds and the water in a blender and blend on high for several minutes, until the mixture is opaque white.

3. Line a strainer with a double thickness of cheesecloth and place the strainer over a 2-quart bowl.

4. Pour the blended mixture into the strainer and let all the liquid drain off. Then gather the edges of the cheesecloth and twist to squeeze all the almond milk out of the cheesecloth. Discard the cheesecloth.

5. Flavor the almond milk however you'd like, and shake before serving.

6. Almond milk should be stored in an airtight container in the refrigerator and consumed within several days.

PER SERVING Calories: 40, Protein: 1g, Total Carbohydrates: 2g, Fiber: 1g, Total Fat: 4g, Saturated Fat: 0g, Cholesterol: 0mg, Sodium: 140mg

Turkish Coffee Almond Frappé

Serves 2   Prep time: 10 minutes

QUICK & EASY | VEGAN | GLUTEN-FREE   If you love iced sweet coffee drinks, this drink is for you! Here's a rich coffee-flavored drink without all the extra sugar and flavorings that go into the coffeehouse version. I love this drink as an afternoon pick-me-up on a warm day. Turkish coffee can be found online or in Mediterranean or specialty grocery stores. Instant espresso is available in many grocery stores.

2½ cups cold Almond Milk (page 38)

¼ cup pure maple syrup or
    4 pitted dates

1 tablespoon ground Turkish
    coffee or 2 teaspoons instant
    espresso powder

Ice (optional)

❋ You can customize this drink however you'd like by adding vanilla, cinnamon, or whole unsalted almonds, or even unsalted almond butter.

1. In a blender, combine the almond milk, maple syrup or dates, coffee, and ice (if using). Blend until smooth.

2. Pour into two glasses and serve immediately.

PER SERVING Calories: 153, Protein: 1g, Total Carbohydrates: 29g, Fiber: 1g, Total Fat: 5g, Saturated Fat: 0g, Cholesterol: 0mg, Sodium: 209mg

Moroccan Mint Tea

Serves 4   Prep time: 15 minutes

QUICK & EASY | VEGAN | GLUTEN-FREE | BIG 8 ALLERGEN-FRIENDLY   This tea is served all over Morocco, sweet, minty, and piping hot. It's a great digestive after a meal. In Morocco it's served with much flourish, poured from a great height, but don't worry if you can't master that technique; it's good no matter how it's poured.

1 tablespoon green tea leaves

¼ cup sugar

4 cups boiling water

1 bunch fresh mint, washed

✳ Make a batch, strain it into a quart jar, and chill overnight to make iced Moroccan mint tea. Serve in tall glasses garnished with fresh mint sprigs.

1. Place the tea leaves and sugar in a teapot. Add boiling water.

2. Add the mint, press it down into the water with a spoon, and let steep at least 5 minutes.

3. Pour the tea through a strainer to serve.

PER SERVING Calories: 48, Protein: 0g, Total Carbohydrates: 13g, Fiber: 0g, Total Fat: 0g, Saturated Fat: 0g, Cholesterol: 0mg, Sodium: 1mg

Chamomile Lemon Honey Iced Tea

Serves 4   Prep time: 10 minutes

QUICK & EASY | VEGETARIAN | GLUTEN-FREE | BIG 8 ALLERGEN-FRIENDLY   Chamomile tea was a standard in my childhood. It was used to cure all ills and as a rinse to keep blond highlights in my hair when I was little. Even though hot chamomile tea with honey and lemon is a time-honored cure for a sore throat, I like it iced to drink with lunch or tapas.

4 bags high-quality chamomile tea
¼ cup lemon juice
¼ cup honey
4 cups boiling water
4 strips lemon peel
Ice cubes

❋ Orange juice and peel can be used instead of the lemon juice and peel for a sweeter drink. Replace the honey with pure maple syrup for a vegan drink.

1. Place the chamomile, lemon, and honey in a teapot. Pour boiling water over them, and let steep for at least 5 minutes.

2. Remove the tea bags and pour the tea into a heat-tempered jar or pitcher. Chill until cold.

3. When you're ready to serve, twist strips of lemon peel to release the oils and place one strip in each serving glass. Add ice and the iced tea.

PER SERVING Calories: 68, Protein: 0g, Total Carbohydrates: 18g, Fiber: 0g, Total Fat: 0g, Saturated Fat: 0g, Cholesterol: 0mg, Sodium: 4mg

Pomegranate Berry Sangria

Serves 4   Prep time: 10 minutes

QUICK & EASY | VEGETARIAN | GLUTEN-FREE | BIG 8 ALLERGEN-FRIENDLY   Pomegranates grow throughout the Middle East, and the ruby-red tart juice is the perfect backdrop for sangria. Pomegranate juice is combined here with red wine and berries, resulting in an anti-oxidant powerhouse! It's also a good way to use up an opened bottle of wine. If you have any sangria left over, freeze it in a shallow tray and mash it with a fork to make granita. It makes a lovely dessert on a hot evening.

4 cups pomegranate juice

1 cup red wine

⅓ cup honey

¼ cup lemon juice

1 cup mixed berries

4 strips orange peel

❀ I like to serve this over ice. I also like to add a cinnamon stick to the pitcher as it chills, but I remove it to serve, since the cinnamon flavor can become too strong. To make it vegan, use sugar instead of honey.

1. Place the pomegranate juice, red wine, honey, lemon juice, and berries in a large serving pitcher.

2. Stir to dissolve the honey and slightly mash the berries. Chill.

3. When you're ready to serve, twist the orange peel to release the oils and place a strip of peel in each glass. Pour in the sangria and serve.

PER SERVING Calories: 299, Protein: 1g, Total Carbohydrates: 65g, Fiber: 1g, Total Fat: 0g, Saturated Fat: 0g, Cholesterol: 0mg, Sodium: 17mg

Raspberry Fizz Cocktail

Serves 4   Prep time: 10 minutes

QUICK & EASY | VEGAN | GLUTEN-FREE | BIG 8 ALLERGEN-FRIENDLY   Muddled raspberries are the base for this cocktail, which is topped with mint and Prosecco—a light, frothy Italian sparkling wine. It's great for brunch, or for an afternoon pick-me-up with an assortment of tapas.

1 pint raspberries

2 tablespoons reduced-sugar
   raspberry jam

1 tablespoon lemon juice

2 teaspoons chopped fresh mint

1 bottle Prosecco, chilled

❋ You can crush the berries hours ahead, or store the macerated berries in an ice cube tray in the freezer and use them frozen in this cocktail. If you can't find Prosecco in your area, any champagne or sparkling wine will work.

1. Reserve 8 to 12 nice berries to float in wine glasses.

2. Place the remaining berries, raspberry jam, and lemon juice in a small bowl.

3. Using the back of a spoon or a pestle, mash the berries to release their juices and macerate them.

4. Place around 2 tablespoons of the mashed berries in each glass.

5. Add a pinch of chopped mint to each glass.

6. Gradually add the Prosecco, pouring slowly so it doesn't overflow.

7. Stir once and serve.

PER SERVING Calories: 204, Protein: 1g, Total Carbohydrates: 18g, Fiber: 5g, Total Fat: 1g, Saturated Fat: 0g, Cholesterol: 0mg, Sodium: 2mg

three

Breakfast

Watermelon with Ricotta and Mint

Serves 4   Prep time: 15 minutes

QUICK & EASY | VEGETARIAN | GLUTEN-FREE   In Greece most of the hotels offer substantial breakfast buffets, including large platters of cut melon and seasonal fruits. Watermelon always appeals to me on those hot summer mornings, especially when I eat it with creamy ricotta cheese. The cold, juicy watermelon is the perfect balance to the dense, high-protein ricotta.

6 cups watermelon cubes

¼ cup lemon juice

¼ cup honey

2 cups ricotta cheese

Freshly ground black pepper
   (optional)

2 tablespoons chopped
   fresh mint

❋ The watermelon, lemon juice, and honey can be combined the night before to save time in the morning.

1. Place the watermelon in a large bowl and add the lemon juice and honey. Mix gently to combine.

2. Divide the watermelon among four serving dishes.

3. Top each dish with ½ cup ricotta cheese.

4. Freshly grind pepper over each serving (if using). Sprinkle with chopped mint, and serve immediately.

PER SERVING Calories: 309, Protein: 16g, Total Carbohydrates: 42g, Fiber: 1g, Total Fat: 10g, Saturated Fat: 6g, Cholesterol: 38mg, Sodium: 163mg

Yogurt with Honey, Seeds, and Raspberries

Serves 4   Prep time: 10 minutes

QUICK & EASY | VEGETARIAN | GLUTEN-FREE   Yogurt and honey is the standard breakfast throughout much of the Mediterranean. In the regions where strained yogurt is the norm, it is sliced from a loaf and drizzled with honey. It's thick and creamy and packed with protein. Fortunately high-protein Greek yogurt is readily available, and topped with honey, fruit, and seeds, it's a delicious breakfast.

1 quart (4 cups) plain Greek yogurt
½ cup honey
1 pint raspberries
½ cup sunflower, flax, pumpkin, or chia seeds or a combination of seeds

✻ To make this dish vegan, replace the yogurt with vegan yogurt and replace the honey with pure maple syrup.

1. Divide the yogurt among four serving dishes.

2. Drizzle honey over the yogurt.

3. Add the raspberries and seeds, and serve.

PER SERVING Calories: 377, Protein: 16g, Total Carbohydrates: 62g, Fiber: 6g, Total Fat: 7g, Saturated Fat: 3g, Cholesterol: 15mg, Sodium: 175mg

Muesli with Apricots and Pistachios

Serves 4   Prep time: 15 minutes

QUICK & EASY | VEGAN   Oats and oatmeal aren't a mainstay of Mediterranean cooking. A breakfast grain mixture would most likely comprise rolled barley, wheat, or buckwheat. Of these three grains, barley and wheat have gluten in them. If you're avoiding gluten, feel free to make this dish entirely out of rolled oats or buckwheat. Apricots can be dried, frozen, or fresh if you make this when they are in season.

2 cups rolled barley, wheat, buckwheat, or a combination of all three

1½ cups Almond Milk (page 38)

½ cup chopped dried apricots or 1 cup chopped fresh or frozen apricots

¼ cup honey

1 tablespoon lemon zest

1 teaspoon ground cinnamon

¼ cup chopped unsalted pistachios

❈ To make this without nuts, replace the almond milk with rice milk and omit the pistachios. To make it vegan, use pure maple syrup instead of honey.

1. In a medium bowl, stir together the grains, almond milk, apricots, honey, lemon zest, and cinnamon.

2. Cover and refrigerate overnight.

3. The next morning, divide the muesli among four serving bowls and top with pistachios.

PER SERVING Calories: 371, Protein: 8g, Total Carbohydrates: 54g, Fiber: 8g, Total Fat: 3g, Saturated Fat: 0g, Cholesterol: 0mg, Sodium: 99mg

Breakfast Polenta

Serves 4 to 6   Prep time: 10 minutes   Cook time: 10 minutes

QUICK & EASY | VEGAN | GLUTEN-FREE | BIG 8 ALLERGEN-FRIENDLY   Cornmeal is inexpensive and easily found in most parts of the world, and just about every culture makes both porridge and bread with it. In America, we call polenta "grits." And just like grits, you can make it sweet and creamy or savory. I like to make it plain so I can add toppings however the mood hits me. If you use instant polenta, you will decrease the cooking time by several minutes. If your market doesn't sell polenta, substitute cornmeal or grits.

6 cups water

2 teaspoons salt

1¾ cups instant polenta, cornmeal, or grits

4 tablespoons extra-virgin olive oil

❋ Here are a few simple ways to use this basic dish. To make it sweet, drizzle with honey and serve with a dollop of yogurt or a splash of Almond Milk (page 38), and top with fruit. To make it savory, add chopped herbs and grated Parmesan cheese, and serve with a fried egg on top.

1. Place the water in a medium pot and bring to a boil.

2. Add the salt and slowly whisk in the polenta.

3. Continue to cook and stir the polenta over medium heat until it's thick and the grain is tender and no longer crunchy, about 5 minutes.

4. Stir in the olive oil.

5. Ladle into bowls and serve.

6. Basic polenta can be made ahead, refrigerated well-wrapped, and reheated as needed. It can also be spooned into a loaf pan, and once cool, sliced into thick slices to pan-fry in olive oil and served.

PER SERVING Calories: 172, Protein: 1g, Total Carbohydrates: 10g, Fiber: 2g, Total Fat: 15g, Saturated Fat: 2g, Cholesterol: 0mg, Sodium: 1314mg

Whole-Grain Toast with Herbed Goat Cheese and Tomatoes

Serves 4   Prep time: 15 minutes

QUICK & EASY | VEGETARIAN   Thick slices of country-style whole-wheat bread are toasted, rubbed with garlic, spread with herbed goat cheese, and topped with slices of tomato. It's important to use a hearty whole-grain rustic loaf–whatever is available in the freshly baked section of your market. Traditional sliced bread won't work as well. This breakfast will transport you to a Tuscan village. Don't forget the espresso!

4 thick slices Italian-style whole-grain country bread

5 ounces goat cheese, at room temperature

1 tablespoon chopped fresh chives

1 tablespoon chopped fresh basil

1 garlic clove, smashed

¼ cup extra-virgin olive oil

1 large ripe tomato, cut into thick slices

1 teaspoon sea salt

¼ teaspoon freshly ground black pepper

❊ If you don't like goat cheese, you can use ricotta or yogurt cheese instead. Yogurt cheese, called labneh, is just yogurt with the liquids strained out.

1. Toast the bread.

2. While it's toasting, mix together the goat cheese, chives, and basil in a small bowl. Set aside.

3. Rub each piece of toasted bread with the smashed garlic clove, and brush each piece of bread with olive oil.

4. Spread the goat cheese mixture on each slice and top with the tomato.

5. Sprinkle each piece of toast with salt and pepper, and serve.

PER SERVING Calories: 342, Protein: 15g, Total Carbohydrates: 13g, Fiber: 2g, Total Fat: 26g, Saturated Fat: 11g, Cholesterol: 37mg, Sodium: 701mg

Smoked Mackerel on Brown Bread with Spinach

Serves 4   Prep time: 10 minutes   Cook time: 5 minutes

QUICK & EASY   You may be thinking, mackerel for breakfast? Yes, and it's delicious, a change from smoked salmon, and loaded with healthy fats. Adding spinach to this open-faced sandwich gives you a strong, healthy start to your day. Smoked mackerel can be found in the fish department in most markets, either with the smoked salmon or canned, where you find the tuna.

4 slices dark rye bread

2 teaspoons Dijon mustard

1 cup packed baby spinach

12 thin slices cucumber

1 tablespoon chopped scallions

6 ounces smoked mackerel

¼ teaspoon salt (optional)

¼ teaspoon freshly ground black pepper (optional)

✳ If you can't find smoked mackerel, you can substitute smoked salmon or trout, or use good-quality canned tuna instead.

1. Toast the bread.

2. Spread each toasted slice with the mustard.

3. Arrange baby spinach over the bread and top with the cucumber slices and scallions.

4. Divide the mackerel among the four slices of bread. Sprinkle with the salt and pepper (if using), and serve.

PER SERVING Calories: 143, Protein: 11g, Total Carbohydrates: 18g, Fiber: 2g, Total Fat: 3g, Saturated Fat: 1g, Cholesterol: 10mg, Sodium: 1245mg

Olive Oil Zucchini Muffins

Makes 12   Prep time: 15 minutes   Cook time: 20 minutes

VEGETARIAN   Olive oil is wonderful in baking. It gives baked goods a tender texture and just a hint of olive in the flavor. The orange zest and walnuts add complexity. Because these muffins are so moist, they freeze well and don't dry out. Serve them warm with fresh fruit and yogurt for breakfast, or take one to work for a midmorning snack.

Nonstick cooking spray
1½ cups shredded zucchini
2 eggs
¼ cup honey
3 tablespoons extra-virgin olive oil
1 tablespoon orange zest
1 teaspoon pure vanilla extract
1 cup whole-wheat flour
1 cup almond flour
2 teaspoons baking powder
1 teaspoon baking soda
1 teaspoon ground cinnamon
1 teaspoon salt
½ cup chopped walnuts
   (optional)

❋ This recipe can be made gluten-free by substituting oat or rice flour for the wheat flour. Make it vegan by substituting pure maple syrup for the honey and making vegan "eggs" by combining 2 tablespoons ground flaxseed with ⅓ cup water. Just leave out the nuts if they are a problem for you.

1. Preheat the oven to 375°F.

2. Spray a 12-muffin pan with nonstick cooking spray.

3. In a medium bowl, combine the zucchini, eggs, honey, and olive oil and stir well.

4. Add the orange zest, vanilla extract, wheat and almond flours, baking powder, baking soda, cinnamon, and salt, and mix well.

5. Fold in the chopped walnuts (if using).

6. Scoop the batter by ½-cup scoops into the prepared muffin pan.

7. Bake 15 to 20 minutes or until the muffins are lightly browned. Cool 5 minutes in the pan and remove.

8. Store muffins in a tightly sealed container for several days at room temperature, or freeze for several months.

PER SERVING Calories: 163, Protein: 2g, Total Carbohydrates: 17g, Fiber: 2g, Total Fat: 9g, Saturated Fat: 1g, Cholesterol: 27mg, Sodium: 311mg

Baked Eggs

Serves 4   Prep time: 10 minutes   Cook time: 5 to 10 minutes

QUICK & EASY | VEGETARIAN | GLUTEN-FREE   Baked eggs are a nice change from fried or poached eggs, and are easy to make with a toaster oven. It's best to make them in a low-sided ramekin or gratin dish large enough to hold just two eggs. This way, they will cook more evenly.

4 teaspoons extra-virgin olive oil
8 eggs
½ cup grated Parmesan cheese
1 teaspoon salt
¼ teaspoon freshly ground
    black pepper

❋ Baked eggs can be dressed up by adding roasted vegetables to the dish or using feta or goat cheese instead of Parmesan cheese.

1. Preheat the oven or toaster oven to 400°F.

2. Place 1 teaspoon of olive oil in each of four ramekins, and tilt to coat the ramekin with the oil.

3. Carefully break two eggs into each ramekin.

4. Divide the Parmesan cheese among the four ramekins.

5. Season each ramekin with salt and pepper.

6. Bake the eggs for 5 to 10 minutes, depending on how runny or hard you like your yolks. Serve immediately.

PER SERVING Calories: 212, Protein: 16g, Total Carbohydrates: 1g, Fiber: 0g, Total Fat: 17g, Saturated Fat: 5g, Cholesterol: 337mg, Sodium: 836mg

Chard and Feta Frittata

Serves 6   Prep time: 15 minutes   Cook time: 25 minutes

VEGETARIAN | GLUTEN-FREE   I love to make a frittata when I have bits and pieces of ingredients around the house that I have to use up. I can make it ahead and reheat it in the morning for a fast and easy way to start the day–complete with lots of protein and vegetables.

1 tablespoon extra-virgin olive oil

1 bunch chard, stems removed, leaves coarsely chopped

1 teaspoon salt

¼ teaspoon freshly ground black pepper

¼ cup chopped roasted red peppers

¼ cup chopped olives

1 teaspoon dried oregano

12 eggs, well-beaten

2 ounces crumbled feta cheese

❋ You can make these as individual muffins for an easy grab-and-go meal. Instead of cooking the vegetables in the pie plate in the oven, sauté them first in a frying pan on top of the stove. Divide the vegetables among an oiled 6-muffin pan, top with the beaten eggs and feta, and bake at 375°F for 15 to 20 minutes. Let them cool in the muffin pan about 5 minutes, and then remove by running a knife around the edges. Remove promptly, or they may stick to the muffin pan.

1. Preheat the oven to 375°F.

2. Place the olive oil in a 9-inch deep-sided pie plate.

3. Add the chopped chard, the salt, and the pepper.

4. Place the chard in the oven and cook 10 to 15 minutes, or until the chard is wilted.

5. Remove from the oven and sprinkle the roasted red pepper, olives, and oregano over the chard.

6. Carefully pour the beaten eggs into the pie plate. Scatter the feta over the eggs.

7. Return the pie plate to the oven and bake for 20 to 25 minutes, or until the eggs are just set and they still jiggle a bit when moved.

8. Let it cool for 5 minutes before serving. Cut into wedges and serve.

9. The frittata will last, covered in the refrigerator, for one week. You can freeze frittatas for several months, but when thawed they have a tendency to be runny.

PER SERVING Calories: 184, Protein: 13g, Total Carbohydrates: 3g, Fiber: 1g, Total Fat: 14g, Saturated Fat: 5g, Cholesterol: 336mg, Sodium: 722mg

Herbed Omelet with Balsamic Tomatoes

Serves 2   Prep time: 10 minutes   Cook time: 5 to 10 minutes

QUICK & EASY | VEGETARIAN | GLUTEN-FREE   The trick to making this simple, classically French dish is to cook omelets on a medium flame and slightly undercook the eggs, since they will continue to cook as they rest. The balsamic tomatoes here are a fast and easy sauce that can also be used for pasta, seafood, or poultry.

FOR THE OMELET

4 eggs

1 tablespoon chopped fresh chives

1 tablespoon chopped fresh flatleaf parsley

1 teaspoon chopped fresh tarragon

4 teaspoons extra-virgin olive oil, divided

1 teaspoon salt

¼ teaspoon freshly ground black pepper

FOR THE BALSAMIC TOMATOES

1 tablespoon extra-virgin olive oil

½ pint cherry tomatoes, cut in half

2 teaspoons balsamic vinegar

1 teaspoon salt

¼ teaspoon freshly ground black pepper

¼ teaspoon sugar

❋ If you aren't comfortable flipping the omelet, here's an alternative method. Once the eggs are almost set, turn the heat off and let the omelet sit a minute longer. Then roll the omelet onto the serving plate.

MAKE THE OMELET

1. Whisk the eggs until well blended.

2. Whisk in the chives, parsley, and tarragon.

3. Place 2 teaspoons of olive oil in an omelet pan over high heat, and add half the egg mixture.

4. Tilt the pan to evenly coat with the egg mixture, lower the flame to medium, and cook until the omelet is set on the bottom.

5. Carefully loosen the edges of the omelet with a flexible spatula, slip the spatula underneath, and flip the omelet. Cook for about 1 minute on the other side, and roll the omelet onto a serving dish. Add half the salt and pepper.

6. Make the second omelet. Keep the omelets warm while making the sauce.

MAKE THE BALSAMIC TOMATOES

1. Put the olive oil in the same skillet that the omelets were cooked in. When the oil is hot, add the tomatoes.

2. Add the balsamic vinegar and sauté about 2 minutes.

3. Add the salt, pepper, and sugar, and sauté 1 minute longer.

4. Divide the tomatoes between the two omelets and serve.

PER SERVING Calories: 288, Protein: 12g, Total Carbohydrates: 5g, Fiber: 1g, Total Fat: 25g, Saturated Fat: 5g, Cholesterol: 327mg, Sodium: 2455mg

four

Tapas & Side Dishes

Cucumber Yogurt Salad with Dill

Serves 4   Prep time: 10 minutes

QUICK & EASY | VEGETARIAN | GLUTEN-FREE   I first found this easy and versatile salad years ago in a *Gourmet* magazine cookbook. It's a classic combination that appears in the Mediterranean and throughout northern Europe. It is a cooling addition to a tapas table, but also works well as a side dish for grilled meats and fish.

2 medium cucumbers, peeled and thinly sliced

2 teaspoons salt, divided

1 cup plain Greek yogurt

1 garlic clove, minced

2 scallions, thinly sliced

1 tablespoon extra-virgin olive oil

1 tablespoon lemon juice

1 tablespoon chopped fresh dill

❊ It's best to use Greek yogurt in this recipe, since Greek yogurt is strained and very thick. Even after salting the cucumbers, there will still be a lot of liquid left in them. If you can't find Greek yogurt, a combination of yogurt and sour cream will also work.

1. Place the sliced cucumbers in a strainer, sprinkle them with 1 teaspoon of salt, and set the strainer over a bowl for about 10 minutes, so that the cucumbers release some of their liquid.

2. Pat the cucumbers dry with paper towels and place them in a medium bowl.

3. Add the remaining 1 teaspoon of salt, yogurt, garlic, scallions, olive oil, lemon juice, and dill, and mix well.

4. Serve immediately, or store in an airtight container in the refrigerator. This salad is best if eaten within 2 days, because as the cucumbers sit, it becomes watery and loses flavor.

PER SERVING Calories: 103, Protein: 5g, Total Carbohydrates: 11g, Fiber: 1g, Total Fat: 5g, Saturated Fat: 1g, Cholesterol: 4mg, Sodium: 581mg

Mashed Garbanzo Beans and Tahini

Serves 4   Prep time: 15 minutes

QUICK & EASY | VEGAN | GLUTEN-FREE | BIG 8 ALLERGEN-FRIENDLY   In this classic Lebanese twist on hummus, the garbanzo beans (also known as chickpeas) are mashed instead of puréed, giving the dish a satisfying, somewhat lumpy texture. Tahini is made from ground toasted sesame seeds. You can find it in the international foods aisle in many supermarkets.

1 (15-ounce) can garbanzo beans, drained and rinsed

⅔ cup tahini

¼ cup extra-virgin olive oil, plus more to drizzle over the top

¼ cup lemon juice

2 garlic cloves, minced

2 teaspoons salt

2 tablespoons chopped fresh flatleaf parsley

¼ teaspoon red pepper flakes (optional)

❋ Add or subtract garlic as you please. Some people like it garlicky and some people like just a hint.

1. Place the garbanzo beans and tahini in a medium bowl. Using a potato masher, mash the mixture until the beans are coarsely mashed.

2. Add the olive oil, lemon juice, garlic, and salt, and mix well. If mixture is too thick, thin it with a little water.

3. Spoon the dip into a serving bowl and top with parsley and pepper flakes (if using).

4. Drizzle with olive oil and serve with Toasted Pita Wedges (page 186) and/or cut-up vegetables.

5. The dip will last about 10 days stored in an airtight container in the fridge.

PER SERVING Calories: 422, Protein: 10g, Total Carbohydrates: 22g, Fiber: 7g, Total Fat: 34g, Saturated Fat: 5g, Cholesterol: 0mg, Sodium: 1393mg

Tabbouleh

Serves 4 to 6   Prep time: 30 minutes

QUICK & EASY | VEGAN   Tabbouleh is worth making at home; you can never get the tartness of the lemon, the fruitiness of the olive oil, the nuttiness of the cracked wheat, and the freshness of the herbs from something bought from a deli case. Since this salad doesn't require cooking, it's a good recipe to make on a hot day.

1 cup boiling water

1 cup fine cracked wheat (bulgur)

½ cup chopped fresh flatleaf parsley

½ cup chopped fresh mint

2 scallions, thinly sliced

2 tomatoes, diced

1 cucumber, peeled, seeded, and diced

¼ cup extra-virgin olive oil

¼ cup lemon juice

1 teaspoon salt

¼ teaspoon freshly ground black pepper

1. Place the boiling water and cracked wheat in a medium bowl and let it sit for 20 minutes for the wheat to soften and absorb the water.

2. Add the parsley, mint, scallions, tomatoes, cucumber, olive oil, lemon juice, salt, and pepper, and mix well.

3. Spoon into a serving dish and serve immediately.

✽ If you'd like to make this ahead, you can soak the cracked wheat the day before, and prep the chopped herbs, onions, tomatoes, and cucumber. Refrigerate the cracked wheat and the vegetables and herbs in separate containers. When you're ready to serve, combine the cracked wheat with the herbs and vegetables and add the olive oil, lemon juice, salt, and pepper right before serving.

PER SERVING Calories: 264, Protein: 6g, Total Carbohydrates: 34g, Fiber: 9g, Total Fat: 14g, Saturated Fat: 2g, Cholesterol: 0mg, Sodium: 604mg

Boiled Artichokes with Aioli

Serves 4   Prep time: 15 minutes   Cook time: 20 minutes

VEGAN | GLUTEN-FREE | BIG 8 ALLERGEN-FRIENDLY   Growing up in California, we had fresh artichokes all spring and summer. We were even able to grow them in our backyard. I like to serve these artichokes stuffed with salad for lunch. Olive oil can replace the aioli, if you'd like.

2 large artichokes
1 garlic clove, smashed
2 teaspoons salt
½ cup Aioli (page 206)

❋ Artichokes are a challenge to prepare, because the tips of their leaves are quite spiny and sharp. It's easier to cut them in half lengthwise, since the leaves can slide while you're trying to cut them. Then I remove the inedible choke—the furry center with purple leaves.

1. Using a sharp chef's knife or serrated knife, cut the artichokes in half lengthwise from the stem end through the top.

2. Using a sharp knife, cut the choke out of the artichokes.

3. Place the garlic clove and salt in a large pot, and cover with enough water to cover the artichokes by 1 inch.

4. Cover the pot and bring to a boil. Boil 20 to 30 minutes, or until the artichokes are tender at the stem end.

5. Remove the artichokes to a serving platter and allow to cool. Drain.

6. Serve the artichokes warm or cold.

7. Serve the artichokes with aioli for dipping the leaves, but be sure and eat the stem, too–that's where most the nutrition is.

8. Cooked artichokes will last 1 week, covered, in the refrigerator.

PER SERVING Calories: 205, Protein: 3g, Total Carbohydrates: 10g, Fiber: 4g, Total Fat: 18g, Saturated Fat: 3g, Cholesterol: 0mg, Sodium: 527mg

Moroccan Carrot Salad with Cinnamon

Serves 4   Prep time: 10 minutes   Cook time: 10 minutes

QUICK & EASY | VEGAN | GLUTEN-FREE | BIG 8 ALLERGEN-FRIENDLY   The cinnamon brings out the natural sweetness in carrots. This dish is at its best when served warm, but can be enjoyed room temperature as well.

3 tablespoons extra-virgin olive oil

2 large carrots, peeled and thinly sliced

1 garlic clove, crushed

1 teaspoon salt

¼ teaspoon freshly ground black pepper

½ teaspoon ground cinnamon

3 tablespoons orange juice

❄ If you're serving this dish cold, add a dollop of Greek yogurt to make a creamy salad.

1. Place a large skillet over high heat. Add the olive oil, and when it is hot, add the carrots.

2. Add the crushed garlic and sauté about 10 minutes, or until the carrots are tender.

3. Add the salt, pepper, cinnamon, and orange juice, and cook 1 minute longer.

4. Spoon into a serving dish and serve.

5. This salad can be made several days ahead and kept covered in the fridge.

PER SERVING Calories: 112, Protein: 1g, Total Carbohydrates: 5g, Fiber: 1g, Total Fat: 10g, Saturated Fat: 2g, Cholesterol: 0mg, Sodium: 606mg

Turkish Bean Salad

Serves 4   Prep time: 15 minutes   Cook time: 50 minutes

VEGAN | GLUTEN-FREE | BIG 8 ALLERGEN-FRIENDLY   If you think you don't like green beans, you've never had them cooked this way. The long, slow cooking with onions and tomatoes bring out a sweet, nutty flavor in the beans.

⅓ cup extra-virgin olive oil
1 white onion, chopped
1 garlic clove, chopped
1 pound green beans, trimmed
    and cut in half
4 Roma tomatoes, chopped
2 teaspoons sugar
1 teaspoon salt
¼ teaspoon freshly ground
    black pepper
3 tablespoons chopped fresh mint
Lemon wedges for garnish

❋ Traditionally this dish is served with dollops of Greek yogurt on top.

1. Place the olive oil in a large pot over high heat.

2. When the oil is hot, add the onion and garlic and sauté 5 minutes, or until the onions are soft and translucent.

3. Add the green beans, tomatoes, sugar, salt, and pepper, then cover and let stew over medium heat about 45 minutes, stirring occasionally. The beans are done when they are very soft.

4. Remove the beans to a serving dish and garnish with chopped mint and lemon wedges. Serve warm or at room temperature.

5. Stewed beans will last about 1 week stored covered in the refrigerator, or can be kept for several months well wrapped in the freezer.

PER SERVING Calories: 222, Protein: 4g, Total Carbohydrates: 18g, Fiber: 6g, Total Fat: 17g, Saturated Fat: 2g, Cholesterol: 0mg, Sodium: 593mg

Greens in Tomato Sauce with Olives

Serves 4 to 6   Prep time: 10 minutes   Cook time: 17 minutes

QUICK & EASY | VEGAN | GLUTEN-FREE | BIG 8 ALLERGEN-FRIENDLY   Lots of people love tomato sauce, but not so many love greens. My husband is one of those people. He will eat anything in tomato sauce, though, so I serve greens this way, and then I can get some greens into him.

1 tablespoon extra-virgin olive oil

1 onion, thinly sliced

1 garlic clove, minced

1½ cups tomato sauce

½ cup red wine

10 ounces baby spinach or other greens

½ cup chopped fresh flatleaf parsley

¼ cup chopped Kalamata olives

1 teaspoon sugar

1 teaspoon salt

¼ teaspoon freshly ground black pepper

❋ Ladle this dish into bowls and add some fried eggs for a delicious breakfast. It's also delicious topped with Parmesan cheese.

1. Place the olive oil in a large skillet over high heat.

2. Add the onion and garlic and sauté for 5 minutes to soften the onions.

3. Add the tomato sauce and red wine and simmer 10 minutes.

4. Add the spinach, parsley, olives, sugar, salt, and pepper and simmer an additional minute or two, or until the greens are wilted.

5. Spoon into a bowl and serve with thick slices of country bread.

6. This dish will last about 1 week tightly covered in the fridge, or can be frozen for several months. It is best served slightly warm.

PER SERVING Calories: 121, Protein: 4g, Total Carbohydrates: 13g, Fiber: 4g, Total Fat: 5g, Saturated Fat: 1g, Cholesterol: 0mg, Sodium: 1199mg

Roasted Carrots with Anise

Serves 4   Prep time: 10 minutes   Cook time: 15 minutes

QUICK & EASY | VEGAN | GLUTEN-FREE | BIG 8 ALLERGEN-FRIENDLY   Anise pairs beautifully with the intense flavor of roasted carrots—and also aids digestion. The vinegar and olive oil help caramelize the carrots, and the onions bring depth of flavor. These are delicious served at room temperature and make a great side dish for roast chicken or pork.

4 large carrots, peeled and cut on
    the diagonal into 1-inch pieces
1 onion, thinly sliced
¼ cup extra-virgin olive oil
1 tablespoon balsamic vinegar
1 tablespoon lemon juice
2 teaspoons sugar or honey
1 teaspoon salt
1 teaspoon whole star anise,
    crushed slightly
¼ teaspoon freshly ground
    black pepper

❋ Served warm, this dish is wonderful topped with a dollop of Greek yogurt.

1. Preheat the oven to 400°F.

2. Place the carrots, onion, olive oil, balsamic vinegar, lemon juice, sugar, salt, anise, and pepper in a medium bowl. Stir to make sure all the ingredients are evenly coated.

3. Pour onto a rimmed baking sheet and roast about 15 to 20 minutes, stirring halfway through. Roast until the carrots are brown around the edges.

4. This is a make-ahead recipe, lasting at least 1 week tightly covered in the refrigerator or for several months in the freezer.

PER SERVING Calories: 158, Protein: 1g, Total Carbohydrates: 12g, Fiber: 2g, Total Fat: 13g, Saturated Fat: 2g, Cholesterol: 0mg, Sodium: 633mg

Patatas Bravas

Serves 4 to 6   Prep time: 10 minutes   Cook time: 55 minutes

VEGETARIAN | GLUTEN-FREE | BIG 8 ALLERGEN-FRIENDLY   One of the best dishes at any tapas bar is patatas bravas. Typically, they are thick chunks of deep-fried potato served with aioli. To lighten the dish, we'll bake the potatoes and serve them with Romanesco Sauce (page 147).

5 medium russet potatoes

⅓ cup extra-virgin olive oil

2 teaspoons salt

1 teaspoon paprika

¼ teaspoon freshly ground
   black pepper

1 recipe Romanesco Sauce
   (page 147) or Aioli (page 206)

❋ The whole potatoes can be baked days ahead and kept in the refrigerator until you are ready to complete the dish. Once made into Patatas Bravas, it's best to eat them fresh.

1. Preheat the oven to 375°F.

2. Wash the potatoes, place them on a baking sheet, and bake until tender, about 35 to 45 minutes.

3. Allow to cool several minutes until you can handle them, and cut them into 8 wedges. Place the wedges in a bowl.

4. Increase the heat to 400°F.

5. Add the olive oil, salt, paprika, and pepper, and mix gently to coat the wedges with the spice mix without mashing the potatoes.

6. Arrange the potatoes in a single layer on a baking sheet.

7. Return the potatoes to the oven and roast 10 to 15 minutes, or until the potatoes are golden brown and crispy.

8. Serve warm with Romanesco Sauce (page 147) or Aioli (page 206).

PER SERVING Calories: 328, Protein: 5g, Total Carbohydrates: 42g, Fiber: 7g, Total Fat: 17g, Saturated Fat: 3g, Cholesterol: 0mg, Sodium: 1179mg

Roasted Eggplant with Pomegranate and Feta

Serves 4 to 6   Prep time: 15 minutes   Cook time: 15 minutes

QUICK & EASY | VEGETARIAN | GLUTEN-FREE   Traditionally the eggplant is fried for this dish, but I roast mine. It's a lot simpler, faster, and makes less of a mess. Pomegranates are only available in the winter, but some markets sell frozen pomegranate seeds year-round. There isn't a good substitution for pomegranate seeds, but if they're not available, chopped toasted walnuts work well in this dish.

1 large eggplant, peeled and cut into ½-inch slices
3 teaspoons salt, divided
½ cup extra-virgin olive oil
2 tablespoons balsamic vinegar
1 tablespoon lemon juice
¼ teaspoon freshly ground black pepper
¼ cup pomegranate seeds
2 ounces feta cheese, crumbled
¼ cup chopped fresh flatleaf parsley

✽ Getting seeds out of a pomegranate can be a challenge, but I've discovered a new way that works pretty well. Roll the whole pomegranate back and forth along a work surface to loosen the seeds. Cut the pomegranate in half around the equator. Hold one half the pomegranate cut side down over a small bowl. With a wooden spoon, vigorously whack the skin side of the pomegranate; this will knock all the loosened seeds into the bowl (be careful, of course, to not hit your hand holding the pomegranate with the spoon!). Do the same to the remaining half of pomegranate. You can store the seeds covered in the refrigerator for about 1 week.

1. Preheat the oven to 400°F.

2. Place the eggplant in a single layer on a baking sheet, sprinkle on both sides with 2 teaspoons of salt, and let it sit for 10 minutes. This gets rid of the excess liquid in the eggplant.

3. While the eggplant sits, combine the olive oil and balsamic vinegar in a small bowl.

4. After 10 minutes, wipe the salt and extra liquid off the eggplant with paper towels.

5. Brush both sides of the eggplant with the oil-vinegar mixture. Return to the baking sheet.

6. Roast until browned on one side, about 5 to 7 minutes. Turn the eggplant and brown the other side, an additional 5 to 7 minutes. Remove the eggplant from the oven and arrange on a serving dish.

7. Drizzle the lemon juice over the eggplant, add the remaining 1 teaspoon salt and the pepper. Sprinkle the pomegranate seeds, feta, and parsley over the top and serve.

8. The roasted eggplant will last about 5 days tightly covered in the refrigerator. Dress and garnish just before serving.

PER SERVING Calories: 295, Protein: 3g, Total Carbohydrates: 10g, Fiber: 4g, Total Fat: 29g, Saturated Fat: 6g, Cholesterol: 13mg, Sodium: 745mg

One Pot Ratatouille

Serves 4 to 6   Prep time: 15 minutes   Cook time: 45 minutes

VEGAN | GLUTEN-FREE | BIG 8 ALLERGEN-FRIENDLY   Ratatouille is a classic French Provençal dish. A true ratatouille involves cooking each vegetable separately and then combining them in one pot for a final simmer. As you can imagine, this takes a lot of time. This recipe cooks everything in one large pot, which simplifies the process a lot. I love ratatouille with herbes de Provence, but if you can't find that mixture in the market, a touch of rosemary will do.

2 Japanese eggplants, cut into ½-inch-thick slices

1 teaspoon salt

¼ cup extra-virgin olive oil

2 garlic cloves, sliced

1 onion, sliced

1 red bell pepper, cored, seeded, and cut into ½-inch pieces

4 medium tomatoes, cored and cut into ½-inch pieces

2 large zucchini, cut into ½-inch slices

¼ cup chopped fresh flatleaf parsley

1 tablespoon capers

1 teaspoon herbes de Provence or rosemary

1 teaspoon salt

¼ teaspoon freshly ground black pepper

❋ Japanese eggplants are small, long eggplants, and are used in this dish because they are easier to work with. If you can't find Japanese eggplants, buy a small eggplant and cut it into 1-inch cubes.

1. Sprinkle the Japanese eggplant with salt and set it aside in a colander in the sink while you prepare the rest of the vegetables. This draws the excess water from the eggplant.

2. In a large Dutch oven or a heavy pot with a lid, heat the olive oil over high heat.

3. Add the garlic, onion, and bell pepper and sauté for about 8 minutes or until the vegetables are wilted.

4. Dry the eggplant with a paper towel and add the eggplant, tomatoes, and zucchini to the pot.

5. Bring to a simmer and cook, stirring the vegetables for about 5 minutes. Cover the pot, reduce the heat to medium, and continue to cook on a low simmer for about 30 minutes or until the vegetables are very soft and tender.

6. Remove the pot from the heat and add the parsley, capers, herbes de Provence, salt, and pepper.

7. Spoon into a serving dish and serve.

8. Ratatouille is a hearty dish that can be stored in an airtight container in the refrigerator for about 1 week or in the freezer for several months.

PER SERVING Calories: 250, Protein: 7g, Total Carbohydrates: 32g, Fiber: 15g, Total Fat: 14g, Saturated Fat: 2g, Cholesterol: 0mg, Sodium: 825mg

Olive Oil-Roasted Root Vegetables with Dill

Serves 4 to 6   Prep time: 10 minutes   Cook time: 20 minutes

QUICK & EASY | VEGETARIAN | GLUTEN-FREE | BIG 8 ALLERGEN-FRIENDLY   I like to make a big pan of roasted vegetables on the weekend to enjoy throughout the week. Root vegetables are particularly delicious cooked this way because their natural sugars brown nicely when baked. When I'm tired of eating them as vegetables, I throw them in a pot with some broth, bring them to a boil, purée the soup, and add a dollop of yogurt.

4 carrots, peeled and cut into ½-inch slices

2 parsnips, peeled and cut into ½-inch slices

4 large beets, peeled and cut into ½-inch cubes

1 large sweet potato, peeled and cut into ½-inch cubes

1 red onion, cut into ½-inch dice

⅓ cup extra-virgin olive oil

2 tablespoons balsamic vinegar

1 tablespoon honey

2 teaspoons salt

¼ teaspoon freshly ground black pepper

1 tablespoon chopped fresh dill

✳ The time it takes for the vegetables to cook will depend on the freshness of the vegetables. If they are still too crunchy after 20 minutes in a hot oven, cover them with foil and bake an additional 10 to 15 minutes. The foil will help the vegetables steam, which will cook them through.

1. Preheat the oven to 375°F.

2. Combine the carrots, parsnips, beets, sweet potato, red onion, olive oil, balsamic vinegar, honey, salt, and pepper in a large bowl and mix well.

3. Divide the vegetables between two rimmed baking sheets and place them in the oven.

4. Roast 10 minutes, stir the vegetables, and roast until the vegetables are tender and slightly browned, an additional 10 to 14 minutes.

5. Scoop into a serving dish, add the dill, and serve.

6. You can store roasted vegetables in the refrigerator for about 5 days.

PER SERVING Calories: 333, Protein: 4g, Total Carbohydrates: 45g, Fiber: 9g, Total Fat: 17g, Saturated Fat: 2g, Cholesterol: 0mg, Sodium: 1308mg

Sweet and Sour Pumpkin with Pine Nuts and Raisins

Serves 4   Prep time: 15 minutes   Cook time: 30 minutes

VEGAN | GLUTEN-FREE   The raisin and pine nut partnership shows up in many dishes throughout the Mediterranean. It's often paired with chard or other greens, as a garnish on a bulgur pilaf, or over fish. In this North African dish, it is served with pumpkin, which adds a nutty sweetness to the dish. This dish is good warm or at room temperature.

¼ cup extra-virgin olive oil

1 large onion, thinly sliced

4 cups peeled and seeded pumpkin or any winter squash, cut into 1-inch cubes

1 teaspoon salt

½ teaspoon freshly ground black pepper

2 teaspoons sugar or honey

2 teaspoons red wine vinegar

1 teaspoon ground cinnamon

¼ cup raisins

¼ cup pine nuts (pignoli), toasted

❁ Peeling winter squash can be difficult. I've found the best method is to use a very sharp vegetable peeler. Many stores sell peeled, cubed butternut squash, which is perfect in this recipe.

1. Place a large Dutch oven or a heavy pot with a lid over high heat. Add the olive oil and onion and sauté until the onions are soft, about 5 minutes.

2. Add the pumpkin and sauté over medium heat for 5 minutes.

3. Add the salt, pepper, sugar, vinegar, cinnamon, and raisins, then cover and cook over low heat, stirring occasionally, for 20 minutes or until the squash is tender.

4. Spoon the pumpkin into a serving dish, sprinkle the pine nuts over the top, and serve.

5. Without the pine nuts, this dish can be stored in the fridge for about 1 week and in the freezer for several months. To keep the crunch of the pine nuts, add them right before serving.

PER SERVING Calories: 301, Protein: 5g, Total Carbohydrates: 34g, Fiber: 9g, Total Fat: 19g, Saturated Fat: 3g, Cholesterol: 0mg, Sodium: 597mg

Oven-Fried Artichoke Hearts

Serves 4   Prep time: 15 minutes   Cook time: 15 minutes

QUICK & EASY | VEGETARIAN | GLUTEN-FREE | BIG 8 ALLERGEN-FRIENDLY   I love this recipe because it's fast, easy, and can be made ahead and heated when ready to serve. You can serve the artichokes plain or with a drizzle of Aioli (page 206), or drizzled with olive oil and a generous squeeze of lemon.

¾ cup cornmeal

⅓ cup finely grated Parmesan cheese

1 teaspoon garlic powder

1 teaspoon salt

½ teaspoon dried rosemary

½ teaspoon paprika

¼ teaspoon freshly ground
    black pepper

½ cup extra-virgin olive oil, divided

2 eggs, lightly beaten

1 (14-ounce) can artichoke hearts,
    drained

❋ This dish can be made ahead. However, as the artichokes cool, they lose their crunch. It's best to crisp them in the oven on a baking sheet before serving.

1. Preheat the oven to 400°F.

2. In a wide, shallow bowl, combine the cornmeal, Parmesan cheese, garlic powder, salt, rosemary, paprika, and pepper. Mix well.

3. Combine ¼ cup olive oil and the eggs. Add the drained artichoke hearts to the eggs and stir to combine.

4. Oil a rimmed baking sheet with the remaining ¼ cup olive oil.

5. Remove an artichoke heart from the eggs, roll it in the cornmeal mixture to coat evenly, and place on the prepared baking sheet. Continue until all the artichoke hearts have been coated.

6. Bake the artichokes 15 to 20 minutes, or until lightly browned. Serve hot.

7. The oven-fried artichokes can be stored in the fridge for 1 week, or frozen longer. It's best to store them in a single layer or packed between layers of waxed paper in an airtight container.

PER SERVING Calories: 415, Protein: 12g, Total Carbohydrates: 29g, Fiber: 7g, Total Fat: 31g, Saturated Fat: 6g, Cholesterol: 89mg, Sodium: 813mg

Baked Vegetable Bites Filled with Feta

Serves 4 to 6   Prep time: 20 minutes   Cook time: 30 minutes

VEGETARIAN | GLUTEN-FREE   This recipe looks more complicated than it is. A vegetable mixture is pressed around cubes of feta and baked. It's delicious served warm or cold with Romanesco Sauce (page 147) or Tzatziki (page 210). If you want to reheat already-made vegetable bites, place ¼ cup olive oil in a cast iron skillet over a medium-high flame and brown them about 2 to 3 minutes per side, until they are crisp.

3 tablespoons extra-virgin olive oil, plus more for the pan and to brush the bites

2 cups red lentils

4 cups water

1 bay leaf

1 small onion, chopped

1 carrot, peeled and chopped

1 small potato, peeled and chopped

1 teaspoon paprika

1 teaspoon ground cumin

1 teaspoon salt

¼ teaspoon freshly ground black pepper

1 cup almond meal

1 egg, beaten

1 teaspoon chopped fresh dill

8 ounces feta cheese, cut into ½-inch cubes

❋ If you have the time, it's easier to make the bites if both the lentils and vegetables are at room temperature. To make these vegan, omit the feta and replace the egg with a mixture of 1 tablespoon ground flaxseed combined with 3 tablespoons water.

1. Preheat the oven to 375°F.

2. Brush a baking sheet with olive oil.

3. Place the lentils, water, and bay leaf in a medium pot and bring to a boil. Reduce to a simmer and cook until the lentils are tender, about 10 to 15 minutes. Drain and let cool.

4. Place a large skillet over high heat and add 3 tablespoons olive oil. Add the onion and sauté about 3 minutes to soften.

5. Add the carrot, potato, paprika, cumin, salt, and pepper and cook until the vegetables are just tender.

6. In a food processor, combine the cooled lentils, cooked vegetables, almond meal, egg, and dill. Pulse several times until the mixture starts to stick together but still has texture. If you don't have a food processor, combine the ingredients in a large bowl and mash with a potato masher.

7. Using about ⅓ cup of the mixture, shape into a ball. Make an indentation in the center of the ball, press a cube of feta into the indentation, and press the mixture over the feta to hide the feta completely. Place the ball on the oiled baking sheet.

8. When all the bites have been made (you should end up with 16 to 18), brush them with olive oil and bake them until golden on the top and bottom, about 20 minutes.

9. These can be made ahead and stored in the refrigerator for 5 days, or frozen for several months.

PER SERVING Calories: 544, Protein: 26g, Total Carbohydrates: 45g, Fiber: 18g, Total Fat: 30g, Saturated Fat: 11g, Cholesterol: 91mg, Sodium: 1248mg

five

Soups & Salads

Golden Gazpacho

Serves 4   Prep time: 20 minutes

QUICK & EASY | VEGAN | GLUTEN-FREE | BIG 8 ALLERGEN-FRIENDLY   Gazpacho is a cold vegetable soup served throughout Spain. It is typically made with red peppers and red tomatoes, but I like to make mine with yellow peppers and golden tomatoes, resulting in a sweeter, less acidic soup.

1½ pounds golden tomatoes, cored and cut into 8 wedges

1 cucumber, peeled, seeded, and coarsely chopped

1 yellow bell pepper, seeded and chopped

½ cup chopped red onion

1 small red chile pepper, seeded and chopped (optional)

1 garlic clove, sliced

¼ cup extra-virgin olive oil

2 tablespoons lemon juice

1 teaspoon salt

½ teaspoon ground cumin

½ teaspoon ground turmeric

¼ teaspoon freshly ground black pepper

2 tablespoons finely chopped fresh cilantro

❄ Gazpacho is a wonderful way to enjoy seasonal vegetables. Typically it has tomatoes, cucumbers, and peppers, but you can certainly choose what varieties of these vegetables you use. I like to add grilled jumbo prawns to the soup for a refreshing summer lunch.

1. Place the tomatoes, cucumber, bell pepper, red onion, chile pepper (if using), garlic, olive oil, and lemon juice in a large bowl and mix to combine.

2. In a food processor or blender, purée the vegetables in batches. Gazpacho can be as smooth or as chunky as you'd like.

3. When it's all been puréed, add the salt, cumin, turmeric, and pepper.

4. Ladle into bowls and garnish with chopped cilantro.

5. Gazpacho can be stored in the fridge for about 3 days (any longer and the flavors diminish) or frozen for several months. If freezing, don't add the cilantro since it will lose its fresh flavor; add it when ready to serve.

PER SERVING Calories: 170, Protein: 3g, Total Carbohydrates: 13g, Fiber: 4g, Total Fat: 13g, Saturated Fat: 2g, Cholesterol: 0mg, Sodium: 595mg

Fennel and Leek Broth

Serves 4   Prep time: 10 minutes   Cook time: 15 minutes

QUICK & EASY | VEGAN | GLUTEN-FREE | BIG 8 ALLERGEN-FRIENDLY   This is a simple broth, restorative when you've overindulged and you need a little something to get you back on track. Fennel aids digestion and leeks aid in balancing digestion with magnesium. Fresh turmeric root looks a bit like fresh ginger, but it's bright orange inside. If your supermarket doesn't have it, try an Asian or Latino grocery store. Or you can substitute 1 teaspoon powdered turmeric.

2 large leeks, root and top trimmed,
    thinly sliced
1 large fennel bulb, stemmed
    and thinly sliced
1 garlic clove, thinly sliced
1 carrot, peeled and thinly sliced
1 thin slice fresh turmeric root
6 cups low-sodium vegetable or
    chicken broth
1 teaspoon salt
¼ teaspoon freshly ground
    black pepper
¼ cup chopped fresh flatleaf parsley
2 tablespoons chopped fresh dill
¼ cup extra-virgin olive oil

✳ It's easy to dress this soup up or down. You can add cooked chicken to make it more substantial, or make it creamy with a dollop of yogurt.

1. Place the leeks, fennel, garlic, carrot, and turmeric in a large pot. Add the broth, salt, and pepper.

2. Bring to a boil, then reduce to a simmer. Cook for 5 to 10 minutes, or until the carrots are tender.

3. Ladle the soup into serving bowls and top with the parsley and dill. Drizzle with olive oil and serve.

4. This soup will last in the refrigerator for 1 week, and can be frozen for several months.

PER SERVING Calories: 189, Protein: 5g, Total Carbohydrates: 15g, Fiber: 3g, Total Fat: 13g, Saturated Fat: 2g, Cholesterol: 0mg, Sodium: 742mg

Lemon Almond Soup

Serves 4   Prep time: 15 minutes   Cook time: 15 minutes

QUICK & EASY   This recipe is inspired by the classic Spanish almond soup, which has a base of almonds and breadcrumbs to make a thick broth. I've added some cooked chicken to make it heartier. If you'd rather, cooked salmon would be nice in this soup.

¼ cup extra-virgin olive oil
½ cup blanched (skinless) unsalted almonds
2 cups fresh bread, cut into ½-inch cubes, from a baguette or country bread
4 cups low-sodium chicken broth, divided
2 garlic cloves, sliced
¼ teaspoon saffron threads
1 cup cooked chicken, cut into small pieces
1 teaspoon salt
¼ teaspoon freshly ground black pepper
Zest and juice of 1 lemon
¼ cup chopped fresh flatleaf parsley

❋ You can make this a vegetarian or vegan by using vegetable broth instead of chicken broth and omitting the cooked chicken. You can make this gluten-free by using gluten-free bread.

1. Heat the olive oil in a large Dutch oven or a heavy pot with a lid.

2. Add the almonds and sauté until they are golden. Remove with a slotted spoon to a blender jar.

3. Add the bread cubes to the pot and sauté until lightly toasted. Put about ½ cup of the toasted bread cubes aside to use as garnish and place the rest in the blender jar.

4. Add 2 cups of the chicken broth and the garlic and the saffron to the blender and purée until the mixture is smooth.

5. Return the mixture to the pot and add the remaining 2 cups broth, the cooked chicken, salt, and pepper, and heat until the mixture is warmed through.

6. Add the zest and juice of the lemon.

7. Ladle the soup into serving bowls and top with the reserved toasted bread cubes and the chopped parsley.

8. This soup will last in the refrigerator for several days and in the freezer for several months. If you are making the soup ahead, don't add the reserved toasted bread cubes or the parsley until right before you serve it.

PER SERVING Calories: 316, Protein: 17g, Total Carbohydrates: 16g, Fiber: 2g, Total Fat: 20g, Saturated Fat: 3g, Cholesterol: 27mg, Sodium: 796mg

Roasted Red Pepper Soup with Spinach

Serves 4   Prep time: 15 minutes   Cook time: 15 minutes

QUICK & EASY | VEGETARIAN | GLUTEN-FREE   This deep red, garlic-laced soup is dotted with spinach and garnished with chopped olives. The potato in this recipe gives it a velvety texture. We used to make this soup a lot when I had my restaurant; it was a good winter soup, when produce isn't as abundant. You can make this in a snap and serve it as a first course for dinner.

¼ cup extra-virgin olive oil

1 onion, thinly sliced

2 to 3 garlic cloves, minced

1 (16-ounce) jar roasted red peppers, drained

1 large potato, peeled and cut into ½-inch cubes

4 cups chicken or vegetable broth

1 teaspoon fresh thyme leaves

1 teaspoon salt

¼ teaspoon freshly ground black pepper

1 (5-ounce) bag baby spinach

½ cup chopped green olives

2 ounces feta cheese, crumbled

❋ To make it vegan, use vegetable broth and omit the feta. You can add beans or cooked shrimp to the soup to make it heartier, or add toasted pine nuts or walnuts as a garnish.

1. Heat the olive oil in a large Dutch oven or a heavy pot with a lid.

2. Add the onion and garlic and sauté until they are lightly browned.

3. Add the roasted peppers, potato, broth, thyme, salt, and pepper, and bring to a boil. Reduce to a simmer and cook about 5 to 8 minutes, or until the potatoes are tender.

4. Purée the soup in a blender or with an immersion blender, and return to the pot. Add the spinach and cook an additional 3 to 5 minutes, or until the spinach is wilted.

5. Ladle the soup into bowls and garnish with the chopped olives and feta.

6. This soup can be refrigerated for 1 week and frozen for several months. If you're making it ahead, don't add the olives and feta until you're ready to serve.

PER SERVING Calories: 331, Protein: 9g, Total Carbohydrates: 31g, Fiber: 6g, Total Fat: 20g, Saturated Fat: 5g, Cholesterol: 13mg, Sodium: 1384mg

Garbanzo Bean and Lentil Soup

Serves 4 to 6   Prep time: 15 minutes   Cook time: 15 minutes

QUICK & EASY | VEGAN | GLUTEN-FREE | BIG 8 ALLERGEN-FRIENDLY   Inspired by a Moroccan winter soup, this soup tastes better the next day. Rich, thick, and satisfying, the beans provide plenty of protein. Traditionally the recipe uses dried beans, but that takes a lot of time. This quicker version uses canned beans, which decreases the cooking time significantly.

¼ cup extra-virgin olive oil

1 white onion, thinly sliced

1 (14-ounce) can crushed tomatoes

3 celery stalks, sliced

2 tablespoons tomato paste

1 teaspoon ground ginger

1 teaspoon ground cinnamon

1 (15-ounce) can garbanzo beans,
   drained and rinsed

1 (14-ounce) can lentils, drained

2 zucchini, sliced

1 teaspoon salt

¼ teaspoon freshly ground
   black pepper

Juice of 1 lemon

¼ cup chopped fresh
   flatleaf parsley

¼ cup chopped fresh cilantro

❋ This soup can be dressed up by serving it drizzled with tahini, or with a dollop of yogurt. It is very hearty and will last in the refrigerator for about 10 days, or can be frozen for several months.

1. Heat the olive oil in a large Dutch oven or a heavy pot with a lid.

2. Add the onion and sauté until it is lightly browned.

3. Add the crushed tomatoes, celery, tomato paste, ginger, and cinnamon and simmer, stirring occasionally, about 5 minutes.

4. Add the garbanzo beans, lentils, zucchini, salt, and pepper and simmer about 5 minutes. If the mixture is too thick, thin it with water or broth.

5. Add the lemon juice, parsley, and cilantro and serve.

6. This soup will keep in the refrigerator for about 10 days, or can be frozen for several months. If you're making it ahead, add the lemon, parsley, and cilantro just before serving.

PER SERVING Calories: 466, Protein: 23g, Total Carbohydrates: 64g, Fiber: 26g, Total Fat: 15g, Saturated Fat: 2g, Cholesterol: 0mg, Sodium: 813mg

White Beans with Chicken

Serves 4 to 6   Prep time: 15 minutes   Cook time: 40 minutes

GLUTEN-FREE | BIG 8 ALLERGEN-FRIENDLY   It may be the Greek in me, but I'm not a big fan of traditional chili—which is why this is one of my favorite recipes. In this Mediterranean version of chili, cubes of chicken are sautéed in olive oil and simmered in broth with white beans, vegetables, and rosemary. Serve it with a dollop of yogurt and pita chips.

¼ cup extra-virgin olive oil

4 boneless, skinless chicken breasts, cut into 1-inch pieces

1 onion, chopped

1 fennel bulb, chopped

2 garlic cloves, minced

2 celery stalks, chopped

2 large carrots, peeled and sliced into ¼-inch slices

1 teaspoon salt

¼ teaspoon freshly ground black pepper

1 sprig fresh rosemary

½ teaspoon ground turmeric

4 cups chicken broth

1 (15.5-ounce) can white beans, drained and rinsed

2 tablespoons chopped fresh basil

❋ If you aren't concerned with eating dairy, add ½ cup of Parmesan cheese, which adds a nice saltiness to the beans.

1. Heat the olive oil in a large Dutch oven or a heavy pot with a lid.

2. Add the chicken and brown on each side, about 1 minute per side. Remove the chicken and set aside.

3. Add the onion, fennel, garlic, and celery and sauté until lightly browned, about 7 minutes.

4. Add the carrots, salt, pepper, rosemary, and turmeric and sauté an additional 2 minutes.

5. Return the chicken to the pan and add the broth. Bring to a boil, reduce to a simmer, and cook about 5 minutes, or until the chicken is cooked through.

6. Add the beans and cook an additional minute or so to warm through. Remove the sprig of rosemary, add the chopped basil, and serve.

7. This dish can be made ahead and refrigerated for 5 days or frozen for several months. Add the fresh basil just before serving.

PER SERVING Calories: 579, Protein: 50g, Total Carbohydrates: 47g, Fiber: 12g, Total Fat: 22g, Saturated Fat: 4g, Cholesterol: 101mg, Sodium: 822mg

Chicken and Rice Soup

Serves 4   Prep time: 15 minutes   Cook time: 20 minutes

GLUTEN-FREE | BIG 8 ALLERGEN-FRIENDLY   I use leeks in this recipe instead of onions because they are mellower and sweeter, but if you can't find leeks in your market, you can use onions instead. Soothing and satisfying, chicken and rice soup was one of my mother's cure-alls for whatever ails you.

¼ cup extra-virgin olive oil

2 leeks, root and top trimmed, thinly sliced

1 fennel bulb, chopped

1 garlic clove, sliced

2 carrots, peeled and thinly sliced

½ cup rice

6 cups chicken broth

2 sprigs fresh thyme

1 teaspoon salt

¼ teaspoon freshly ground black pepper

2 cups cooked chicken, cut into ½-inch cubes

Zest and juice of 1 lemon

2 scallions, thinly sliced

❋ To make this soup vegan, use vegetable broth instead of chicken broth and cubes of tofu instead of chicken.

1. Heat the olive oil in a large Dutch oven or a heavy pot with a lid.

2. Add the leeks, fennel, garlic, and carrot and sauté until they are lightly browned.

3. Add the rice and stir to combine.

4. Add the chicken broth, thyme, salt, and pepper and bring to a boil.

5. Reduce to a simmer and cook, covered, for 15 minutes, or until the rice is tender.

6. Add the chicken, lemon zest and juice, and scallions. Remove the thyme sprigs and serve.

PER SERVING Calories: 382, Protein: 27g, Total Carbohydrates: 34g, Fiber: 4g, Total Fat: 15g, Saturated Fat: 3g, Cholesterol: 54mg, Sodium: 793mg

Greens and Herbs Salad

Serves 4   Prep time: 15 minutes

QUICK & EASY | VEGAN | GLUTEN-FREE   This simple and classic French salad makes a lovely first course . . . or a last course, as salads are eaten in France. The base of the salad is butter lettuce; it's dressed lightly with olive oil and lemon, and has a delicate herb flavor.

2 large heads butter or Boston or Bibb lettuce, leaves removed, washed, and dried

2 radishes, thinly sliced

1 tablespoon chopped fresh chives

1 tablespoon chopped fresh flatleaf parsley

2 teaspoons chopped fresh tarragon

¼ cup extra-virgin olive oil

2 tablespoons lemon juice

1 teaspoon lemon zest

1 teaspoon salt

¼ teaspoon freshly ground black pepper

¼ cup chopped toasted walnuts or hazelnuts (optional)

❋ You can prepare the lettuce and radishes and store them for 24 hours in a plastic bag with a paper towel at the bottom to absorb any water that may drop off the leaves. The herbs can be chopped and stored in an airtight container for several hours.

1. Arrange the lettuce leaves in a serving platter or bowl.

2. Top with the radishes, chives, parsley, and tarragon.

3. Drizzle olive oil and lemon juice over the lettuce. Sprinkle on the lemon zest, salt, and pepper and toss gently to coat the lettuce leaves.

4. Sprinkle the toasted nuts over the top (if using), and serve immediately.

PER SERVING Calories: 134, Protein: 1g, Total Carbohydrates: 6g, Fiber: 1g, Total Fat: 13g, Saturated Fat: 2g, Cholesterol: 0mg, Sodium: 593mg

Greek Village Salad

 Good

Serves 4   Prep time: 15 minutes

QUICK & EASY | VEGETARIAN | GLUTEN-FREE   On a menu in Greece this salad is often referred to as Horiatiki Salad. *Horio* is the Greek word for "village," and the ingredients can change from village to village. However, typically it's a large bowl or platter that is loaded with sliced cucumber, tomatoes, olives, and feta. It's placed in the middle of the table for everyone to share. You can keep that tradition when you serve it in your home, or line individual salad dishes with greens and mound the salad ingredients on top.

2 large cucumbers, peeled, seeded, and sliced into ½-inch slices

3 large ripe tomatoes, cored and cut into 8 wedges each

½ red onion, thinly sliced

1 teaspoon salt

¼ teaspoon freshly ground black pepper

¼ cup extra-virgin olive oil, plus more to drizzle over the salad (optional)

2 tablespoons red wine vinegar

½ cup Kalamata olives

4 ounces feta cheese

1 teaspoon dried oregano

✳ Typically, the feta is not crumbled for this salad, but of course feel free to use crumbled feta if you'd prefer. To make ahead, you can place the cucumbers, tomatoes, and onion in an airtight container in the refrigerator overnight. Finish the salad shortly before serving.

1. Arrange the cucumbers on a large serving platter.

2. Add the tomatoes and place the onion slices on top.

3. Sprinkle with the salt and the pepper, and drizzle the olive oil and red wine vinegar over the vegetables.

4. Scatter the olives over the dressed salad and put the brick of feta in the middle. Sprinkle the dried oregano over the feta, drizzle with additional oil (if using), and serve immediately.

PER SERVING Calories: 263, Protein: 7g, Total Carbohydrates: 15g, Fiber: 3g, Total Fat: 20g, Saturated Fat: 6g, Cholesterol: 25mg, Sodium: 1052mg

Arugula with Parmesan and Hazelnuts

Serves 4   Prep time: 15 minutes

QUICK & EASY | VEGETARIAN | GLUTEN-FREE   Arugula is very popular throughout Italy. It has a very small leaves and a peppery taste. It's easy to grow if you're a gardener, and can even be grown in a container. If your market doesn't have arugula, substitute baby spinach.

⅓ cup extra-virgin olive oil

2 tablespoons balsamic vinegar

1 teaspoon Dijon mustard

1 teaspoon salt

¼ teaspoon freshly ground
    black pepper

1 (5-ounce) package arugula

½ cup shaved Parmesan cheese

¼ cup chopped toasted hazelnuts

❋ Hazelnut oil is great in this recipe instead of olive oil. However, nut oils can be expensive and don't last very long. If you want to take the plunge and experiment with hazelnut oil, it can be used instead of olive oil in many of your favorite salad dressings. Buy just a little bit at a time.

1. In a small bowl, whisk together the olive oil, vinegar, mustard, salt, and pepper.

2. Place the arugula in a large bowl, add the dressing, and toss well to combine.

3. Spoon the dressed greens into a large serving bowl and top with shaved Parmesan cheese and toasted hazelnuts.

PER SERVING Calories: 229, Protein: 6g, Total Carbohydrates: 3g, Fiber: 1g, Total Fat: 23g, Saturated Fat: 5g, Cholesterol: 10mg, Sodium: 737mg

Zucchini, Farro, and Pesto Salad

Serves 4   Prep time: 10 minutes   Cook time: 20 minutes

QUICK & EASY | VEGETARIAN   Farro is a whole grain that is enjoyed throughout Italy. It is high in protein and fiber, and has a nutty taste and a toothsome texture. Farro is a form of wheat, so it does have gluten, although some people can tolerate it better than other varieties of wheat. This salad is great served warm or at room temperature.

1 cup farro

2 cups water

2 teaspoons salt, divided

3 tablespoons extra-virgin olive oil

3 medium zucchini, sliced into
¼-inch slices

¼ cup sliced roasted red peppers

2 scallions, thinly sliced

½ cup Pesto (page 209)

¼ teaspoon freshly ground
black pepper

❋ If you are gluten-free, this salad can be made with brown rice instead of farro. If you're vegan, omit the cheese from the pesto recipe.

1. Place the farro, water, and 1 teaspoon of the salt in a medium pot over high heat.

2. Bring to a boil, cover, and reduce to a simmer. Cook for about 15 to 20 minutes, or until the farro is tender and the water is absorbed. Place the cooked farro in a large bowl and set aside.

3. In a large skillet, heat the olive oil. When hot, add the sliced zucchini and sauté until the zucchini is tender and slightly browned. Spoon the zucchini into the bowl with the farro.

4. Add the roasted red peppers, scallions, pesto, 1 teaspoon salt, and the pepper. Mix well and serve immediately.

5. This salad can be stored in the refrigerator for 5 days. If stored any longer, it loses its flavor.

PER SERVING Calories: 354, Protein: 11g, Total Carbohydrates: 39g, Fiber: 5g, Total Fat: 18g, Saturated Fat: 3g, Cholesterol: 4mg, Sodium: 1311mg

Panzanella

Serves 4   Prep time: 15 minutes

QUICK & EASY | VEGAN   This salad was created as a way for people to use up their day-old bread, but it's so delicious that I find myself making it with fresh bread. The basic elements are bread, tomatoes, and basil, but you can be as creative as you like based on what is in season or looks good in the market.

½ loaf baguette or Italian country loaf
   or similar, cut into 1-inch cubes
4 large ripe tomatoes, cored and
   cut into 1 inch cubes
2 garlic cloves, minced
1 bunch fresh basil, chopped
½ cup extra-virgin olive oil
¼ cup red wine vinegar
1½ teaspoons salt
½ teaspoon freshly ground
   black pepper

❋ Some of my favorite add-ins for this recipe are peeled and seeded cucumbers, seeded and sliced red peppers, sliced pepperoncini, and artichoke hearts.

1. Place the bread, tomatoes, garlic, and basil in a large bowl. Stir to moisten the bread with the juice from the tomatoes.

2. Add the olive oil, vinegar, salt, and pepper and mix well.

3. Let it sit for 5 to 15 minutes to allow the flavors develop before serving.

PER SERVING Calories: 395, Protein: 8g, Total Carbohydrates: 35g, Fiber: 4g, Total Fat: 27g, Saturated Fat: 4g, Cholesterol: 0mg, Sodium: 1194mg

Tuna, Tomato, Pepper, Olive, and Egg Salad

Serves 4 to 6   Prep time: 20 minutes

QUICK & EASY | GLUTEN-FREE   This is another version of a salad Niçoise, but unlike a Niçoise, this salad can be mixed together in one bowl. Leftovers make a delicious filling for a sandwich on a ciabatta roll. One of my favorite food memories was eating Niçoise sandwiches in the train station in the south of France. They were huge and would last us two meals.

1 (5-ounce) package baby spinach

2 (5-ounce) cans tuna packed in water, drained

4 medium ripe tomatoes, cored and cut into 1-inch cubes

1 red bell pepper, seeded and thinly sliced

½ red onion, thinly sliced

1 garlic clove, minced

½ cup pitted Niçoise olives

2 hard-boiled eggs, peeled and cut into quarters

2 tablespoons capers

¼ cup extra-virgin olive oil

2 tablespoons red wine vinegar

1 teaspoon salt

¼ teaspoon freshly ground black pepper

1. Place the baby spinach, tuna, tomatoes, bell pepper, onion, garlic, olives, eggs, capers, olive oil, vinegar, salt, and pepper in a large bowl and toss to combine.

2. Let it sit for 5 to 10 minutes before serving to allow the flavors to develop.

3. Place in a serving bowl and serve immediately.

❋ To make this salad ahead, combine the drained tuna, tomato cubes, red pepper slices, red onion slices, minced garlic, pitted olives, peeled and quartered eggs, and capers in one container; and the olive oil, vinegar, salt, and pepper in another. When you're ready to serve, combine the ingredients in the first container and add the dressing.

PER SERVING Calories: 340, Protein: 24g, Total Carbohydrates: 11g, Fiber: 4g, Total Fat: 23g, Saturated Fat: 4g, Cholesterol: 104mg, Sodium: 958mg

Fennel, Grapefruit, and Crab Salad with Parsley Lemon Dressing

Serves 4   Prep time: 15 minutes

QUICK & EASY | GLUTEN-FREE   This lovely, light salad is filled with fresh flavors and is the perfect lunch on a warm day. Fennel, lemon, and parsley are classic flavors throughout the Mediterranean. If you can't find crab, you can substitute bay shrimp or prawns. Or make it with smoked salmon and serve this salad for brunch.

1 head romaine lettuce, washed and chopped

1 fennel bulb, shaved or sliced very thin

1 large pink grapefruit, peeled and cut into ½-inch cubes

1 pound crabmeat

2 teaspoons salt, divided

¼ teaspoon freshly ground black pepper

⅓ cup extra-virgin olive oil

1 shallot, minced

1 teaspoon Dijon mustard

Zest and juice of 1 lemon

2 tablespoons chopped fresh flatleaf parsley

¼ teaspoon red pepper flakes

1. Arrange the lettuce on a large platter, top with the fennel, grapefruit, and crab, and sprinkle with 1 teaspoon of the salt and the pepper.

2. In a small bowl, whisk together the olive oil, shallot, mustard, lemon zest and juice, parsley, 1 teaspoon salt, and the red pepper flakes until well combined.

3. Drizzle the dressing over the salad.

4. Any leftover dressing can be stored in the refrigerator for several days.

❊ To make this salad ahead, you can prep ingredients and store them in the refrigerator. Combine the prepared lettuce and fennel; the grapefruit cubes; crabmeat; and the dressing, 1 teaspoon salt, olive oil, shallot, mustard, lemon zest and juice, and red pepper flakes in separate containers for several hours or up to 24 hours ahead. The dressing can be stored in the refrigerator for several days. The parsley and the additional 1 teaspoon salt can be added when the salad is assembled.

PER SERVING Calories: 294, Protein: 10g, Total Carbohydrates: 27g, Fiber: 3g, Total Fat: 18g, Saturated Fat: 3g, Cholesterol: 23mg, Sodium: 2167mg

six

Wraps & Sandwiches

Caprese Wrap

Serves 4   Prep time: 20 minutes

QUICK & EASY | VEGETARIAN   This is the classic Caprese salad–mozzarella, tomatoes, and basil–tucked into a wrap for a delicious sandwich. The trio of mozzarella, tomatoes, and basil shows up in recipes throughout Italy. The threesome is the core of the Margherita pizza–my favorite–as well as in baked ziti. For a more robust sandwich, this combination is delicious on a ciabatta or French roll.

½ pint cherry tomatoes, cut in half
¼ cup extra-virgin olive oil
1 tablespoon red wine vinegar
1 teaspoon salt
¼ teaspoon red pepper flakes (optional)
¼ cup chopped basil
4 sandwich wraps
6 ounces fresh mozzarella cheese, cut into thick slices, divided

❈ The tomatoes can be prepped ahead and left at room temperature for several hours before making the sandwiches.

1. Place the tomatoes, olive oil, red wine vinegar, salt, red pepper flakes (if using), and basil in a small bowl. Mix well and set aside.

2. Place the sandwich wraps on a work surface.

3. Arrange the mozzarella down the middle of each sandwich wrap.

4. Spoon the tomato-basil mixture over the mozzarella and fold the wrap over the filling.

5. Place seam side down on a plate and allow to rest for 5 to 10 minutes before serving, so the flavors can develop.

6. Roll each wrap tightly and serve.

PER SERVING Calories: 291, Protein: 14g, Total Carbohydrates: 14g, Fiber: 2g, Total Fat: 21g, Saturated Fat: 7g, Cholesterol: 23mg, Sodium: 853mg

Aram Sandwich

Serves 4   Prep time: 30 minutes

QUICK & EASY | VEGAN   These rolled, sliced sandwiches are always a favorite. The beauty of them is you can make them ahead and slice and serve them later. Lavash is an Armenian soft unleavened flatbread that resembles flour tortillas. It's made from very thin dough that's baked in an extremely hot oven and cooks almost immediately. It's sold at many markets in the deli area. If you can't find it, you can make these sandwiches with pita bread.

2 (16- or 18-inch) pieces lavash, round or square

1 cup hummus

1 cup baby spinach

1 cup peeled and thinly sliced cucumbers

½ cup chopped roasted red peppers

¼ cup chopped green olives

½ cup chopped scallions

❋ If you're using pita, warm the bread first to make it pliable. Since pita is thicker than lavash, rolling it will be difficult. I recommend stuffing the pita rather than rolling it. To make a small appetizer-size sandwich, you can use large flour tortillas instead of lavash. Warming them first will make them easier to roll.

1. Place the lavash on a flat work surface.

2. Spread each bread with hummus.

3. Arrange the spinach on the lower third of each bread.

4. Top with cucumbers, roasted peppers, green olives, and scallions.

5. Rolling from the bottom, roll the lavash like a jelly roll.

6. Wrap each roll in plastic wrap and refrigerate until ready to serve, at least 10 minutes.

7. When ready to serve, slice the rolls into 1½- to 2-inch-thick slices. How many slices per serving will depend on what size lavash bread is available.

PER SERVING Calories: 237, Protein: 9g, Total Carbohydrates: 32g, Fiber: 17g, Total Fat: 10g, Saturated Fat: 1g, Cholesterol: 0mg, Sodium: 708mg

Grilled Veggie and Tapenade Wrap

Serves 4   Prep time: 20 minutes

QUICK & EASY | VEGAN   The easiest vegetables to grill are zucchini, peppers, eggplant, fennel, and onions, because they can be sliced thick and grilled without falling through the grate. Feel free to use any vegetable combination that you like. The bread for wraps is found either in the deli section or bread section of the grocery store.

3 zucchini, cut lengthwise into
    ½-inch-thick slices
1 red bell pepper, seeded and
    cut into quarters
1 small red onion, cut into
    ½-inch-thick slices
¼ cup extra-virgin olive oil
4 sandwich wraps
¼ cup Tapenade (page 208)
1 cup baby spinach
¼ cup chopped fresh flatleaf parsley
4 teaspoons lemon juice
1 teaspoon salt
¼ teaspoon freshly ground
    black pepper

❋ There are many gluten-free alternatives to wraps. If you're using a gluten-free bread, it will work best if it's at room temperature, because cold it is too stiff. Grilled chicken, crumbled feta, or goat cheese are all great additions to this sandwich.

1. Heat a grill until hot.

2. Brush the slices of zucchini, bell pepper, and onion with the olive oil. Grill each vegetable until it is marked with the grill on each side, about 2 to 3 minutes per side. Remove the vegetables and cover with foil to allow them to steam for 5 minutes; this makes them more tender.

3. If you do not have an outdoor grill, cook the vegetables the same way on a stovetop grill or in a very hot cast iron skillet.

4. Arrange the wraps on a work surface.

5. Place the grilled vegetables down the middle of the four wraps.

6. Top the vegetables with the tapenade, spinach, parsley, lemon juice, salt, and pepper.

7. Fold the wrap over the filling and place seam side down on a plate to serve.

8. The vegetables can be grilled several days ahead and stored in the refrigerator until you're ready to make the sandwiches.

PER SERVING Calories: 240, Protein: 4g, Total Carbohydrates: 21g, Fiber: 5g, Total Fat: 17g, Saturated Fat: 3g, Cholesterol: 0mg, Sodium: 818mg

Roasted Vegetable and Goat Cheese Sandwich

Serves 4   Prep time: 30 minutes

QUICK & EASY | VEGETARIAN   This is a good way to use up roasted vegetables left over from dinner. If you don't have any, I've included a recipe for quick roasted vegetables below the recipe. It's easier to spread the goat cheese if it's at room temperature.

8 slices whole-grain country bread

2 teaspoons Dijon mustard

2 cups baby spinach

1⅓ cups Olive Oil–Roasted Root Vegetables with Dill (page 69, or quick recipe below)

4 ounces goat cheese, at room temperature

1 tablespoon chopped fresh basil

Juice of ½ lemon

½ teaspoon red pepper flakes (optional)

❃ To make quick roasted vegetables, thinly slice 2 zucchini, 1 red bell pepper, and ½ onion thinly and combine with 3 tablespoons of olive oil, 1 teaspoon salt, and ¼ teaspoon freshly ground black pepper in a medium bowl. Mix well. Spoon the mixture onto a rimmed baking sheet and roast in a 400°F oven for 15 to 20 minutes. You can use the vegetables warm or at room temperature.

1. Place the bread on a work surface in a single layer.

2. Spread four slices with the mustard.

3. Arrange the spinach over each of the four slices.

4. Place about ⅓ cup roasted vegetables over the spinach on each slice.

5. Spread the goat cheese on the remaining four slices of bread.

6. Top each goat cheese-covered piece of bread with the chopped basil, lemon juice, and red pepper flakes (if using).

7. Place the goat cheese-covered bread on top of the bread with the roasted vegetables, cut each sandwich in half, and serve.

PER SERVING Calories: 392, Protein: 18g, Total Carbohydrates: 30g, Fiber: 6g, Total Fat: 23g, Saturated Fat: 9g, Cholesterol: 30mg, Sodium: 950mg

Tomato, Feta, Cucumber, and Tapenade on Ciabatta

Serves 4   Prep time: 15 minutes

QUICK & EASY | VEGETARIAN   I love the chewy texture of ciabatta and how the big air pockets in the bread absorb the juices and seasonings of the vegetables. These sandwiches taste better if they've been sitting awhile, which makes them an ideal make-ahead sandwich. I use English cucumbers in sandwiches, since they have almost no seeds, but any cucumber will do.

4 ciabatta or French rolls

½ cup extra-virgin olive oil

2 tablespoons red wine vinegar

¼ cup Tapenade (page 208)

3 large ripe tomatoes, cored
    and thickly sliced

16 slices English cucumber

4 ounces feta cheese, crumbled

1 teaspoon salt

1 teaspoon dried oregano

¼ teaspoon freshly ground
    black pepper

❀ You can omit the feta to make these sandwiches vegan. Using jarred tapenade is fine if you don't have the time to make it.

1. Cut the ciabatta rolls in half.

2. Brush one half of each ciabatta with olive oil and vinegar.

3. Spread about 1 tablespoon of tapenade on the seasoned half of each ciabatta roll.

4. Place three or four slices of tomato over the tapenade.

5. Top with four slices of cucumber, and divide the crumbled feta over the cucumbers.

6. Sprinkle each sandwich with the salt, oregano, and pepper.

7. Top each with the other half of the ciabatta roll and let the sandwiches sit for about 15 minutes (or up to 3 hours) before serving.

PER SERVING Calories: 450, Protein: 9g, Total Carbohydrates: 24g, Fiber: 3g, Total Fat: 36g, Saturated Fat: 8g, Cholesterol: 25mg, Sodium: 1104mg

Tuscan Tuna Pita

Serves 4   Prep time: 20 minutes

QUICK & EASY   The combination of tuna, white beans, and peppers is very common throughout the Mediterranean. Canned and drained white beans will work just fine. Pepperoncini are pickled small green peppers; they aren't very hot and they provide a lot of tangy flavor. In this recipe the ingredients are packed into a pita pocket for easy eating. You can also leave out the pita entirely; the filling is a great salad on its own. The filling for the pitas can be made several days ahead, but the sandwiches can't be stuffed until shortly before serving, since they will quickly get soggy.

4 large fresh whole-wheat pita breads

1 cup shredded romaine lettuce

2 (5-ounce) cans tuna packed
    in water, drained

1 cup cooked white beans

¼ cup chopped roasted red peppers

½ cup chopped red onion

¼ cup Pesto (page 209)

¼ cup chopped pepperoncini

1 tablespoon red wine vinegar

1 teaspoon salt

¼ teaspoon freshly ground
    black pepper

1. Cut each pita bread in half across the middle.

2. Tuck the shredded romaine in the bottom of each pita half; this helps keep the pitas open when you are ready to stuff them.

3. In a medium bowl, combine the tuna, white beans, roasted peppers, red onion, pesto, pepperoncini, vinegar, salt, and pepper.

4. Stuff the pitas with the salad mixture and serve.

❋ If you don't have pesto handy, you can omit it and use 1 tablespoon of olive oil to moisten the salad and add flavor. Pita bread must be fresh or it will easily fall apart. If your pitas aren't fresh, sprinkle them with water, wrap them in foil, and place them in a warm oven for about 5 minutes to make them soft enough to work with. To make your own pita bread from scratch, check out the recipe for Pork Souvlaki with Tzatziki on Pita Bread on page 102.

PER SERVING Calories: 465, Protein: 33g, Total Carbohydrates: 54g, Fiber: 9g, Total Fat: 14g, Saturated Fat: 3g, Cholesterol: 26mg, Sodium: 1085mg

Zucchini, Mushroom, and Manchego Panini

Serves 4   Prep time: 15 minutes   Cook time: 10 minutes

QUICK & EASY | VEGETARIAN   Panini are grilled sandwiches available throughout Europe, often listed on a menu as "toast." They are made with a two-sided grill that is either electric or used on a stovetop. If you don't have a panini machine, grill these sandwiches in a skillet. The zucchini and mushrooms can be cooked ahead. For best results, let them come to room temperature before making the panini. You can prep the panini by assembling them ahead and grilling them when you're ready to serve.

8 slices country Italian bread or
　　ciabatta rolls, cut in half
2 teaspoons Dijon mustard
¼ cup extra-virgin olive oil
2 zucchini, sliced in ¼-inch slices
8 large mushrooms, sliced
1 teaspoon salt
¼ teaspoon red pepper flakes
　　(optional)
2 cups baby spinach
4 ounces manchego cheese,
　　thinly sliced or shaved

❋ Manchego is a hard sheep's milk cheese from Spain. If you can't find manchego, you can substitute another hard, tangy cheese, such as asiago. Or if you don't like sheep's milk cheese, feel free to substitute Swiss cheese. Pair these panini with the Greens and Herbs Salad (page 83) and a crisp glass of white wine for an easy supper.

1. Place the bread in a single layer on a work surface.

2. Spread four slices with mustard.

3. Place a large skillet over high heat. When the pan is hot, add the olive oil, zucchini, mushrooms, salt, and red pepper flakes (if using). Sauté until the vegetables are tender, about 5 to 7 minutes.

4. Divide the vegetables among the four slices of bread.

5. Top with the spinach and slices of cheese.

6. Top with the remaining slice of bread and place each sandwich in a hot panini maker or skillet and grill until the bread is golden, the spinach has wilted, and the cheese is melted. Serve immediately.

PER SERVING Calories: 313, Protein: 12g, Total Carbohydrates: 16g, Fiber: 3g, Total Fat: 24g, Saturated Fat: 9g, Cholesterol: 30mg, Sodium: 921mg

Prosciutto and Fresh Mozzarella Panini

Serves 4   Prep time: 15 minutes   Cook time: 10 minutes

QUICK & EASY   This is a classic Italian panini. Italian panini are typically a thin sandwich without a lot of filling. Fresh mozzarella really makes this sandwich something special. Most markets sell fresh mozzarella; it's usually sold in the cheese department in pint containers packed in water or brine. If you can't find fresh mozzarella, buy the best mozzarella you can.

8 slices country Italian bread or
ciabatta rolls, cut in half
½ cup Pesto (page 209)
2 tablespoons red wine vinegar
6 ounces prosciutto, thinly sliced
½ pound fresh mozzarella, drained
and sliced
2 cups arugula
1 teaspoon salt
¼ teaspoon red pepper flakes
(optional)

❋ Prosciutto is an Italian style cured ham that is sliced paper thin. It's typically sold in the deli or luncheon meat section of the market. If it's unavailable, substitute thinly sliced ham or turkey.

1. Place the bread in a single layer on a work surface.

2. Spread pesto on all eight slices.

3. Sprinkle vinegar on four slices.

4. Divide the prosciutto among four slices of bread.

5. Place the mozzarella on top of the prosciutto.

6. Top with arugula and sprinkle each sandwich with the salt and red pepper flakes (if using). Top with the remaining slice of bread.

7. Place on a hot panini maker or skillet and grill until the bread is golden brown, the arugula is wilted, and the cheese is melted. Serve immediately.

PER SERVING Calories: 417, Protein: 30g, Total Carbohydrates: 15g, Fiber: 1g, Total Fat: 26g, Saturated Fat: 10g, Cholesterol: 60mg, Sodium: 1747mg

Lamb Mint Sliders

Serves 4   Prep time: 15 minutes   Cook time: 15 minutes

QUICK & EASY   Lamb is frequently eaten throughout the Mediterranean, often ground and shaped around a skewer for easy grilling. I love lamb skewers, but prefer to used those classic flavors to make sliders, which are easier to make–the meat is shaped into small patties to be cooked on the stove. Combined with mint mayonnaise, a slice of tomato, and thinly sliced red onions, it's absolutely delicious.

8 small round dinner rolls or mini hamburger buns

2 pounds ground lamb

1 garlic clove, minced

1 tablespoon balsamic vinegar

1 teaspoon salt

¼ teaspoon freshly ground black pepper

½ cup mayonnaise

2 tablespoons chopped fresh mint

8 slices Roma tomatoes

8 thin slices red onion

❋ Greek yogurt can replace the mayonnaise in this recipe. This recipe uses Roma tomatoes since they have a circumference that matches a small roll, but any tomato will be fine.

1. Cut each roll in half.

2. In a medium bowl, combine the lamb, garlic, vinegar, salt, and pepper. Mix well and shape the mixture into eight small patties.

3. Heat a stovetop grill or large frying pan until hot. If using a frying pan, oil the pan lightly before cooking the lamb patties.

4. Place the lamb patties on the grill (or in the pan) and cook, without crowding, about 3 to 4 minutes per side or until the meat is dark golden on both sides.

5. Let the patties rest while you make the mint mayonnaise.

6. In a small bowl, combine the mayonnaise and mint and stir well.

7. Spread the mint mayonnaise on both sides of each bun. Place a lamb patty on the bottom side of each bun. Top with tomato and red onion slices and serve. Serve 2 sliders per person.

8. The lamb patties can be mixed and formed 1 day ahead and stored in the refrigerator, or frozen longer, uncooked. Thaw before cooking the burgers. The mint mayonnaise can be made 1 day ahead and refrigerated.

PER SERVING Calories: 682, Protein: 69g, Total Carbohydrates: 34g, Fiber: 3g, Total Fat: 29g, Saturated Fat: 8g, Cholesterol: 212mg, Sodium: 1174mg

Pork Souvlaki with Tzatziki on Pita Bread

Serves 4 to 6   Prep time: 90 minutes (less if you buy the pita)   Cook time: 20 minutes

Souvlaki platters are served throughout Greece. Skewered highly seasoned meat is grilled and served on top of hot pita bread topped with thin slices of onions and tomatoes and a dollop of Tzatziki (page 210)–the classic yogurt, cucumber, and mint sauce of the Middle East. This souvlaki can be made with any type of meat. Of course, you can buy pita rather than make it yourself. If you are a novice pita maker, your pita may not puff up on your first try. Don't be discouraged. It's a dance between getting the dough the right texture and thickness and cooking it over a very hot heat. You'll master it with practice.

FOR THE PITA BREAD

1 cup lukewarm water
1 package dry active yeast
½ teaspoon sugar
1 cup whole-wheat flour, divided
1¾ cups all-purpose flour, divided, plus extra for kneading and rolling
1 teaspoon salt
2 tablespoons extra-virgin olive oil

FOR THE SOUVLAKI

1½ pounds pork shoulder, cut into 1-inch pieces
¼ cup extra-virgin olive oil
2 tablespoons red wine vinegar
1 garlic clove, minced
1 teaspoon salt
1 teaspoon dried oregano
6 to 8 skewers

TO ASSEMBLE THE SANDWICHES

½ red onion, thinly sliced
1 large ripe tomato, thinly sliced
1 recipe Tzatziki (page 210)
1 tablespoon minced fresh oregano

MAKE THE PITA BREAD

1. Place the water, yeast, and sugar in a medium bowl and stir to combine.

2. Add ¼ cup whole-wheat flour and ¼ cup all-purpose flour and whisk until smooth.

3. Place the bowl in a warm spot and let rest 15 minutes.

4. Add the salt, olive oil, and remaining ¾ cup whole-wheat flour and ¾ cup all-purpose flour, and mix until the mixture begins to turn into a wet sticky dough. Gradually add more all-purpose flour and knead the dough until it makes a soft, sticky dough. You may not need all the flour.

5. Turn the dough out onto a lightly floured work surface and knead the dough until it's smooth, elastic, and slightly sticky.

6. Return to the bowl, cover with plastic wrap, and leave in a warm spot to double in bulk, about 1 hour.

7. After the dough has risen, preheat the oven to 425°F. Punch the dough down and cut it into six equal pieces. Shape each piece into a ball, cover with plastic wrap, and let rest about 10 minutes.

8. Place a large heavy-duty baking sheet in the hot oven. While the baking sheet is heating, roll each piece of dough into a flat round, about ⅛ inch thick.

9. Remove the hot baking sheet, quickly place three of the rolled pitas on the sheet, and return it to the oven. After 2 to 3 minutes, the dough should puff up. Flip the pitas and cook the other side an additional 2 to 3 minutes. Remove the cooked pitas to a towel-lined plate to keep them warm.

10. Repeat the process with the remaining pita breads.

MAKE THE SOUVLAKI

1. Place the pork, olive oil, red wine vinegar, garlic, salt, and oregano in a medium bowl, cover, and let marinate at least 30 minutes or longer.

2. Preheat a grill or broiler to high.

3. Thread the meat on skewers. Place the meat on the grill or broiler and cook until golden brown on all sides, about 3 to 4 minutes per side.

ASSEMBLE THE SANDWICHES

1. Place a warm pita on a serving plate.

2. Remove the souvlaki from a skewer and place it on top of the pita bread.

3. Top with red onions, tomatoes, and tzatziki. Garnish with oregano and serve immediately.

❋ This recipe can seem overwhelming! You don't have to make your own pita bread. Substitute store-bought pita or naan bread and warm it in the oven just before assembling the sandwich. The souvlaki can marinate overnight. The tzatziki sauce can be made ahead and kept for several days in the refrigerator. The pita bread dough can be made ahead and stored in the refrigerator overnight. If you make the dough ahead, let it sit at room temperature for 30 minutes before shaping it into pitas.

PER SERVING Calories: 1082, Protein: 55g, Total Carbohydrates: 80g, Fiber: 4g, Total Fat: 58g, Saturated Fat: 17g, Cholesterol: 159mg, Sodium: 2515mg

seven

Pizza & Pasta

Mushroom Pesto Pita Pizza

Serves 4   Prep time: 15 minutes   Cook time: 10 to 15 minutes

QUICK & EASY | VEGETARIAN   Pita bread makes a fast and easy substitute for pizza crusts. If you have the ingredients prepped ahead and keep pita in the freezer, you can throw together a pizza in no time.

¼ cup extra-virgin olive oil

12 large mushrooms, sliced

1 teaspoon salt

¼ teaspoon red pepper flakes (optional)

4 whole-wheat pita breads

½ cup Pesto (page 209)

½ cup shredded Parmesan cheese

✳ This pizza can be made with gluten-free pita bread. To make it vegan, replace the pesto with a simple mixture of ½ cup olive oil, one garlic clove, 5 basil leaves, and ½ teaspoon salt puréed in a blender. Spread this over the pita instead of the pesto, and omit the Parmesan cheese. If you want to make your pita bread from scratch, check out the recipe for Pork Souvlaki with Tzatziki on Pita Bread on page 102.

1. Preheat the oven to 375°F.

2. Warm a medium skillet over high heat, then add the olive oil, mushrooms, salt, and red pepper flakes (if using). Sauté until the liquid from the mushrooms has evaporated, about 5 to 7 minutes.

3. Place the pita breads on a baking sheet. Spread the pesto over the pitas and top with the mushrooms and Parmesan cheese.

4. Bake 10 to 15 minutes, or until the pizzas are lightly browned. Serve immediately.

PER SERVING Calories: 474, Protein: 16g, Total Carbohydrates: 40g, Fiber: 6g, Total Fat: 31g, Saturated Fat: 7g, Cholesterol: 18mg, Sodium: 1247mg

White Pizza

Serves 4   Prep time: 15 minutes   Cook time: 10 to 15 minutes

QUICK & EASY | VEGETARIAN   When we think of pizza, we typically think of a bubbling tomato and cheese pie. But in Italy pizza is often a thin crust with a scattering of toppings over thinly sliced cheese—and no tomatoes. I love eating this pizza with a simple salad of greens dressed with extra-virgin olive oil, lemon juice, and a pinch of sea salt.

1 (14- or 16-inch) cooked pizza crust (ideally thin-crust)
1 tablespoon extra-virgin olive oil
8 ounces Fontina cheese, thinly sliced
1 leek, root and top trimmed, thinly sliced
½ fennel bulb, thinly sliced
1 teaspoon salt
1 tablespoon fresh thyme leaves

❋ Fontina cheese is an Italian cow's milk cheese with a delicious buttery flavor. If you can't find Fontina, substitute Swiss or Jarlsberg cheese. The leeks and fennel can be replaced with thinly sliced onion and zucchini.

1. Preheat the oven to 400°F.

2. Place the pizza crust on a large baking sheet. Brush with the olive oil and top with an even layer of cheese.

3. Arrange the sliced leek and fennel on top of the cheese.

4. Sprinkle salt over the toppings and bake about 10 minutes, or until the pizza is lightly browned. Top with thyme leaves.

5. Cooked pizza is best eaten right away. However, you can wrap leftovers in foil and refrigerate it for several days. Reheat in a hot oven or toaster oven for best results.

PER SERVING Calories: 393, Protein: 33g, Total Carbohydrates: 25g, Fiber: 2g, Total Fat: 24g, Saturated Fat: 11g, Cholesterol: 66mg, Sodium: 1055mg

Chicken, Garlic, and Artichoke Pizza with Olives

Serves 4   Prep time: 15 minutes   Cook time: 10 to 15 minutes

QUICK & EASY   Here's a creamy, garlicky pizza with nuggets of cooked chicken and chunks of artichoke hearts and salty olives. Yogurt cheese (from the Yogurt Cheese with Berries recipe on page 195) is the base for this pizza; it's the perfect backdrop for the more robust flavors of the toppings.

1 (14- or 16-inch) cooked pizza crust (ideally thin crust)

1 tablespoon extra-virgin olive oil

8 ounces Yogurt Cheese (page 195)

2 garlic cloves, thinly sliced

3 scallions, thinly sliced

2 cups diced cooked chicken

1 (14-ounce) can artichoke hearts, drained, rinsed, cut in half

½ cup grated Parmesan cheese

½ cup pitted green olives

✳ Yogurt cheese is simply yogurt that has been drained overnight to remove excess whey, leaving behind a thick, velvety cheese similar to cream cheese. If you don't have the time to make yogurt cheese, crumbled goat cheese works well with this recipe.

1. Preheat the oven to 400°F.

2. Place the pizza crust on a large baking sheet. Brush with the olive oil.

3. Top with an even layer of yogurt cheese.

4. Arrange the garlic, scallions, chicken, artichoke hearts, Parmesan cheese, and olives over the top.

5. Bake about 10 minutes or until the pizza is lightly browned.

6. Cooked pizza is best eaten right away. However, you can wrap leftovers in foil and refrigerate it for several days. Reheat in a hot oven or toaster oven for best results.

PER SERVING Calories: 389, Protein: 37g, Total Carbohydrates: 30g, Fiber: 7g, Total Fat: 13g, Saturated Fat: 5g, Cholesterol: 70mg, Sodium: 811mg

Gluten-Free Zucchini and Walnut Pizza

Serves 2   Prep time: 20 minutes   Cook time: 20 minutes

VEGETARIAN | GLUTEN-FREE   This isn't a traditional pizza; the crust is made from ground walnuts and shredded zucchini with a touch of rice flour to help it hold together. You can highly season the walnut-zucchini mixture by doubling the red pepper flakes and oregano and serve it on its own, cut into wedges. Or you can add pizza toppings and return it to the oven.

FOR THE CRUST

¼ cup extra-virgin olive oil, plus
   1 tablespoon to oil the pan
1 cup finely ground walnuts
2 cups shredded zucchini
¼ cup rice flour
1 egg
1 teaspoon salt
¼ teaspoon red pepper flakes
   (optional)
¼ teaspoon dried oregano

FOR THE PIZZA

½ cup sun-dried tomatoes, chopped
½ cup crumbled feta cheese
1 tablespoon chopped fresh basil
1 garlic clove, minced

❋ One cup of ground unsalted almonds or almond flour can be used in place of the ground walnuts. To make this pizza vegan, omit the feta and make an egg substitute by combining 1 tablespoon ground flaxseed with 3 tablespoons water and using this mixture instead of the egg.

MAKE THE CRUST

1. Preheat the oven to 375°F.

2. Brush a 9-inch pie plate with olive oil and set aside.

3. In a medium bowl, combine the walnuts, zucchini, rice flour, egg, olive oil, salt, red pepper flakes (if using), and oregano. Mix well.

4. Press the crust into the prepared pan and bake about 15 to 20 minutes or until the crust is browned around the edges.

5. The cooked crust can be wrapped in plastic wrap and frozen for several months.

MAKE THE PIZZA

1. Top the baked crust with sun-dried tomatoes, feta cheese, basil, and garlic.

2. Return to the oven for 5 minutes to soften the feta.

3. Cut into wedges and serve.

4. Cooked pizza is best eaten right away. However, you can wrap leftovers in foil and refrigerate it for several days. Reheat in a hot oven or toaster oven for best results.

PER SERVING Calories: 862, Protein: 27g, Total Carbohydrates: 36g, Fiber: 8g, Total Fat: 74g, Saturated Fat: 11g, Cholesterol: 107mg, Sodium: 1806mg

Whole-Wheat Roasted Vegetable Pizza with Chèvre

Serves 4   Prep time: 15 minutes   Cook time: 10 minutes

QUICK & EASY | VEGETARIAN   Chèvre is the classic goat cheese of France. It's typically sold in logs that are soft and crumbly. Its mild taste and soft texture make it ideal to cook with. I've included a recipe for whole-wheat pizza dough, but you can buy dough in the freezer section of many markets. The secret to making good pizza is a really hot oven; it's the best way to get a crispy crust.

FOR THE CRUST
1 cup warm water
1 tablespoon sugar
1 tablespoon extra-virgin olive oil
1 envelope rapid-rise yeast
1¾ cups whole-wheat flour
1 cup all-purpose flour, plus more
    to knead and roll the dough
1 teaspoon salt

FOR THE PIZZA
1 tablespoon extra-virgin olive oil
3 cups roasted vegetables from
    Couscous with Roasted Vegetables
    (page 128)
¼ teaspoon red pepper flakes (optional)
2 ounces chèvre, crumbled

❋ It's possible to make this dough with all whole-wheat flour, but it's much more difficult to handle since the gluten in white flour helps add elasticity.

MAKE THE CRUST

1. Place the water, sugar, olive oil, yeast, flours, and salt in the bowl of a food processor or stand mixer and process until the mixture makes a wet dough. Or mix the dough in a large bowl using a wooden spoon. Be sure to mix well.

2. Scrape the dough onto a floured work surface, shape into a round, dust with flour, and let rest 10 minutes.

3. After 10 minutes, flatten the round and gently roll the dough into a 14-inch circle on a floured surface.

4. The dough can be made ahead and kept in the refrigerator overnight, or in the freezer longer. If freezing, thaw the dough overnight in the refrigerator.

MAKE THE PIZZA

1. Preheat the oven to 425°F.

2. Place the dough on a large baking sheet. Brush the top with olive oil.

3. Top with the roasted vegetables, red pepper flakes (if using), and chèvre.

4. Bake 10 to 12 minutes or until the pizza crust is golden. Serve immediately.

5. Cooked pizza is best eaten right away, but you can wrap leftovers in foil and refrigerate them for several days. Reheat in a hot oven or toaster oven for best results.

PER SERVING Calories: 519, Protein: 15g, Total Carbohydrates: 78g, Fiber: 5g, Total Fat: 17g, Saturated Fat: 5g, Cholesterol: 15mg, Sodium: 641mg

Cumin, Lamb, and Pine Nut Pita Pizza

Serves 4   Prep time: 15 minutes   Cook time: 25 minutes

This is one of my favorite flavor combinations—ground lamb and cumin combined with toasted pine nuts and a touch of sweetness from raisins, on a toasted pita bread. If you're not a fan of lamb, feel free to substitute ground chicken or turkey.

1 tablespoon extra-virgin olive oil

1 small onion, chopped

1 garlic clove, chopped

1 pound ground lamb

1 teaspoon ground cumin

½ teaspoon ground cinnamon

½ cup tomato sauce

¼ cup raisins

1 teaspoon salt

¼ teaspoon red pepper flakes (optional)

4 whole-wheat pita breads

¼ cup toasted pine nuts (pignoli)

2 ounces feta cheese, crumbled

¼ cup chopped fresh flatleaf parsley

❈ This topping is delicious on the whole-wheat pizza crust from Whole-Wheat Roasted Vegetable Pizza with Chèvre (page 110). If you want to make your pita bread from scratch, check out the recipe for Pork Souvlaki with Tzatziki on Pita Bread on page 102.

1. Preheat the oven to 375°F.

2. Place a large skillet over high heat. Add the olive oil, onion, and garlic, and sauté until the vegetables are soft, about 5 minutes.

3. Add the lamb and cook until all the pink is gone, about 5 minutes.

4. Add the cumin, cinnamon, tomato sauce, raisins, salt, and red pepper flakes (if using), and simmer an additional 5 minutes, or until most of the liquid in the tomato sauce has evaporated.

5. Place the pita breads on a large baking sheet and divide the lamb mixture among the four pita breads. Top each pita with pine nuts, feta, and parsley.

6. Bake about 10 minutes to heat through and toast the pita. Serve immediately.

7. The lamb filling can be made several days ahead. Keep in an airtight container in the refrigerator.

PER SERVING Calories: 552, Protein: 42g, Total Carbohydrates: 48g, Fiber: 7g, Total Fat: 23g, Saturated Fat: 6g, Cholesterol: 115mg, Sodium: 1332mg

Polenta Lasagna

Serves 6 to 8   Prep time: 30 minutes   Cook time: 30 minutes

VEGETARIAN | GLUTEN-FREE   Layers of polenta create the base for this gluten-free lasagna, and it's easier than working with hot noodles. The polenta creates a canvas for whatever flavors or fillings you want to add. You can use any vegetables, but vegetables that are easy to layer are best, like zucchini, eggplant, mushrooms, peppers, and winter squash.

1 tablespoon extra-virgin olive oil, plus more to oil the pan
1 recipe Breakfast Polenta (page 49)
3 zucchini, thinly sliced
1 teaspoon salt
¼ teaspoon freshly ground black pepper
1 (15-ounce) container ricotta cheese
½ cup sun-dried tomatoes, chopped
3 scallions, thinly sliced
2 garlic cloves, sliced
8 ounces mozzarella cheese, sliced
1 cup grated Parmesan cheese
2 tablespoons chopped fresh rosemary

❋ To make this vegan, omit the ricotta and mozzarella cheese and use 3 to 4 cups of roasted vegetables instead.

1. Preheat the oven to 375°F.

2. Oil a 9-by-13-inch pan.

3. Make the breakfast polenta, and spoon half into the prepared pan. Spread evenly.

4. Heat the olive oil in a large skillet over high heat. Add the zucchini, salt, and pepper, and sauté until the zucchini is tender, about 6 to 7 minutes. Place half the zucchini over the layer of polenta.

5. Using a spoon, spread half the ricotta over the zucchini. Top with half the sun-dried tomatoes, scallions, garlic, mozzarella, Parmesan, and rosemary.

6. Spoon the remaining polenta over the filling, and top with the remaining half of the zucchini, ricotta, sun-dried tomatoes, scallions, garlic, mozzarella, Parmesan, and rosemary.

7. Bake 25 to 35 minutes, or until the lasagna is bubbly and lightly browned.

8. Allow to rest 15 minutes before serving.

9. This can easily be made ahead, up until you bake it, and stored in the refrigerator for several days or the freezer for a few months. For best results, bring it to room temperature before baking.

PER SERVING Calories: 356, Protein: 28g, Total Carbohydrates: 20g, Fiber: 4g, Total Fat: 20g, Saturated Fat: 11g, Cholesterol: 56mg, Sodium: 1863mg

Linguini with Pesto, Spinach, and Olives

Serves 4   Prep time: 15 minutes   Cook time: 10 to 15 minutes

QUICK & EASY | VEGETARIAN   Linguini is fettuccini's smaller, narrower cousin. If you can't find it, fettuccini is fine. This pasta dish is delicious with clams or bay shrimp added. Cook them separately and just mix them in right before serving.

1 pound linguini

3 teaspoons salt, divided

1 tablespoon extra-virgin olive oil, plus more for drizzling

½ cup Pesto (page 209)

2 (5-ounce) bags baby spinach

¼ cup pitted olives, sliced

¼ teaspoon red pepper flakes (optional)

½ cup Parmesan cheese

❋ This recipe can be vegan if you omit the Parmesan cheese from the pesto and the pasta. Any olive will work in this recipe, but green olives are especially good with pesto.

1. Fill a large pot with water and 2 teaspoons salt and bring to a boil. Cook the pasta according to the package directions.

2. Drain the pasta and return it to the pot.

3. Add the olive oil, pesto, spinach, olives, 1 teaspoon salt, and red pepper flakes (if using). Stir until the spinach has wilted. If the spinach doesn't wilt immediately, cover the pot and let it sit on the stove for 5 minutes.

4. Divide the pasta among the serving bowls, top with Parmesan cheese, and drizzle with olive oil. Serve immediately.

5. Leftovers can be stored in the refrigerator for 5 days, or frozen for several months.

PER SERVING Calories: 562, Protein: 23g, Total Carbohydrates: 68g, Fiber: 2g, Total Fat: 23g, Saturated Fat: 6g, Cholesterol: 100mg, Sodium: 1056mg

Whole-Wheat Pasta with Walnuts and Broccolini

Serves 4   Prep time: 15 minutes   Cook time: 10 to 15 minutes

QUICK & EASY | VEGAN   Even though most of the pasta in Italy is made from semolina flour, there are several traditional Italian dishes that are made with whole-wheat pasta, and this is one of them. Whole-wheat pasta has a thicker texture and slightly nutty flavor, which goes nicely with the broccolini and toasted walnuts. I like using broccolini instead of broccoli in this recipe because it's smaller and more tender. However, broccoli also works well.

4 teaspoons salt, divided
1 pound whole-wheat penne
2 bunches broccolini, stems trimmed, cut into 1 inch pieces
1 tablespoon extra-virgin olive oil, plus more for drizzling
1 garlic clove, minced
¼ teaspoon red pepper flakes (optional)
½ cup chopped toasted walnuts

❊ Walnut oil or hazelnut oil is lovely in this dish. Nut oils are a part of the Mediterranean diet; they are minimally processed oils with healthy fats and vitamins. They are expensive and should be used within 1 or 2 months of opening and stored in the refrigerator.

1. Fill a large pot with water and bring to a boil. Once boiling, add 2 teaspoons salt and cook the pasta according to the package directions.

2. Fill a medium pot with water and bring to a boil. Add 1 teaspoon salt and cook the broccolini 5 minutes, or until the vegetables turn a bright green. Drain.

3. Drain the pasta and return to the large pot.

4. Add the olive oil, 1 teaspoon salt, garlic, and red pepper flakes (if using) to the pasta.

5. Add the cooked broccolini and walnuts, drizzle with olive oil, and serve immediately.

6. Leftovers can be stored in the refrigerator for 5 days or frozen for several months.

PER SERVING Calories: 489, Protein: 20g, Total Carbohydrates: 70g, Fiber: 2g, Total Fat: 15g, Saturated Fat: 1g, Cholesterol: 83mg, Sodium: 927mg

Spaghetti with Cherry Tomatoes, Basil, and Cheese

Serves 4 to 6   Prep time: 15 minutes   Cook time: 10 to 15 minutes

QUICK & EASY | VEGETARIAN   Enjoy an uncomplicated, soul-satisfying supper of spaghetti with sautéed tomatoes, basil, and shaved cheese. This is a go-to recipe that my whole family loves. If you don't have cherry tomatoes on hand, it's fine to use chopped tomatoes or sun-dried tomatoes instead. This meal needs nothing more than a glass of wine and a hunk of bread.

3 teaspoons salt, divided

1 pound spaghetti

4 tablespoons extra-virgin olive oil, divided, plus more for drizzling

¼ teaspoon freshly ground black pepper

2 tablespoons butter

1 large shallot, sliced

1 garlic clove, sliced

1 pint cherry tomatoes

¼ cup red wine

¼ teaspoon red pepper flakes (optional)

¼ cup chopped fresh basil

3 to 4 ounces shaved Parmesan cheese

❋ The best way to shave Parmesan cheese is to use a vegetable peeler on a wedge of room-temperature Parmesan cheese. You can also let your guests do this by passing a wedge of cheese and a peeler around the table.

1. Fill a large pot with water and bring to a boil. Once boiling, add 2 teaspoons salt and cook the pasta according to the package directions.

2. Drain and return pasta to the pot. Add 2 tablespoons olive oil, 1 teaspoon salt, and the pepper. Mix well.

3. Place a medium skillet over high heat and add the butter and 2 tablespoons olive oil. When the butter has melted, add the shallots and garlic. Sauté until the vegetables are soft.

4. Add the cherry tomatoes, red wine, and red pepper flakes (if using), and cook about 5 minutes or until the cherry tomatoes start to wrinkle.

5. Place the spaghetti in a serving dish and spoon the cherry tomatoes over the top.

6. Garnish with basil and shaved Parmesan cheese. Drizzle with olive oil and serve.

7. Store leftovers in the refrigerator for up to 4 days.

PER SERVING Calories: 616, Protein: 22g, Total Carbohydrates: 67g, Fiber: 1g, Total Fat: 28g, Saturated Fat: 10g, Cholesterol: 113mg, Sodium: 1018mg

Pasta Primavera

Serves 4   Prep time: 15 minutes   Cook time: 10 to 15 minutes

QUICK & EASY | VEGETARIAN   *Primavera* is Italian for "spring." This pasta dish is bursting with spring vegetables. I like to use asparagus, peas, leeks, and carrots when I make it, but any vegetables will do. I also like to use tarragon instead of basil in this dish–it's not traditional, but I like the flavor combination with the asparagus. And instead of a white wine cream sauce I use yogurt to make it creamy (and much lower in fat). Add the yogurt just before serving, since it will separate if it gets too hot.

3 teaspoons salt, divided

1 pound fettuccini

1 tablespoon extra-virgin olive oil, plus more for drizzling

1 leek, root and top trimmed, thinly sliced

1 bunch asparagus, tough stem ends trimmed, cut into 1-inch pieces

1 cup peas

1 carrot, peeled and thinly sliced

1 garlic clove, minced

¼ teaspoon red pepper flakes (optional)

1 cup plain Greek yogurt

½ cup grated Parmesan cheese

❋ To make this a vegan recipe, omit the yogurt and Parmesan cheese. The vegetables can be made ahead. Just reheat them before adding them to the pasta. Because of the yogurt in the sauce, this dish won't reheat well, so it's best to eat it fresh.

1. Fill a large pot with water and bring to a boil. Once boiling, add 2 teaspoons salt and cook the pasta according to the package directions.

2. While the pasta is cooking, place a large skillet over high heat and add the olive oil and leek. Sauté the leek slices 2 or 3 minutes to soften them.

3. Add the asparagus, peas, carrot, 1 teaspoon salt, garlic, and red pepper flakes (if using). Sauté 5 to 7 minutes or until the vegetables are cooked but still crisp.

4. Drain the pasta and return it to the cooking pot. Add the sautéed vegetables, yogurt, and Parmesan cheese, and mix well.

5. Place in a serving dish and drizzle with extra olive oil before serving.

PER SERVING Calories: 511, Protein: 25g, Total Carbohydrates: 80g, Fiber: 4g, Total Fat: 10g, Saturated Fat: 4g, Cholesterol: 97mg, Sodium: 804mg

Fettuccini with Mushrooms and Fennel

Serves 4   Prep time: 15 minutes   Cook time: 10 to 15 minutes

QUICK & EASY | VEGAN   This recipe uses spinach noodles, which are a lovely bright green color when cooked. They pair nicely with sautéed mushrooms and fennel. Of course, if you can't find spinach pasta, regular pasta will work fine. The mushrooms and fennel are cooked in wine, adding depth of flavor to this dish. I use cremini mushrooms for this recipe, which I think have a bit more flavor than white button mushrooms, but any mushroom will work.

3 teaspoons salt, divided

1 pound spinach fettuccini

3 tablespoons extra-virgin olive oil, plus more for drizzling

2 shallots, thinly sliced

12 large cremini mushrooms, thinly sliced

1 fennel bulb, thinly sliced

¼ teaspoon freshly ground black pepper

1 garlic clove, minced

½ cup white wine

❊ If you aren't vegan, adding a dollop of mascarpone cheese or Greek yogurt to this dish when you serve it adds a lovely creaminess.

1. Fill a large pot with water and bring to a boil. Once boiling, add 2 teaspoons salt and cook the pasta according to the package directions.

2. While the pasta is cooking, place a large skillet over high heat and add the olive oil and shallots. Sauté the shallots 2 to 3 minutes, until softened.

3. Add the mushrooms, fennel, 1 teaspoon salt, the pepper, and garlic, and sauté an additional 5 minutes.

4. Add the wine and simmer until the wine evaporates.

5. Drain the pasta, return it to the cooking pot, and add the sautéed vegetables. Mix well.

6. Place in a serving dish and drizzle with extra olive oil before serving.

7. Leftovers can be stored in the refrigerator for 5 days or frozen for several months.

PER SERVING Calories: 477, Protein: 15g, Total Carbohydrates: 70g, Fiber: 2g, Total Fat: 13g, Saturated Fat: 2g, Cholesterol: 83mg, Sodium: 647mg

Buccatini with Bell Peppers, Zucchini, and Gremolata

Serves 4   Prep time: 15 minutes   Cook time: 10 to 15 minutes

QUICK & EASY | VEGAN   Buccatini is a thick spaghetti-like noodle with a hole down the center, like a straw. I love its toothsome texture and the way it slurps when you eat it. It's available in the dried pasta section of most markets, but if you can't find it, spaghetti or penne both work well in this dish. Gremolata is a classic sauce made of chopped garlic, lemon, and parsley. It's great to have on hand to brighten up just about any dish.

FOR THE PASTA

3 teaspoons salt, divided

1 pound buccatini

1 tablespoon extra-virgin olive oil, plus more for drizzling

1 red bell pepper, seeded and thinly sliced

1 yellow bell pepper, seeded and thinly sliced

3 zucchini, thinly sliced

1 tablespoon capers (optional)

¼ teaspoon red pepper flakes (optional)

½ cup gremolata

FOR THE GREMOLATA

2 garlic cloves, minced

1 bunch flatleaf parsley, stemmed and finely chopped

Zest and juice of 1 lemon

2 teaspoons extra-virgin olive oil

½ teaspoon salt

❄ The vegetables can be sautéed ahead and reheated before adding to the cooked pasta.

MAKE THE PASTA

1. Fill a large pot with water and bring to a boil. Once boiling, add 2 teaspoons salt and cook the pasta according to the package directions.

2. While the water comes to a boil, place the olive oil in a large skillet over high heat.

3. Add the bell peppers, zucchini, and 1 teaspoon salt, and sauté about 10 minutes or until the vegetables are soft.

4. Drain the pasta and put it back in the pot. Add the vegetables, along with the capers and red pepper flakes (if using).

5. Place the pasta in a serving dish, garnish with the gremolata, and drizzle with olive oil.

6. Leftovers can be stored in the refrigerator for 5 days or frozen for several months.

MAKE THE GREMOLATA

1. Combine the garlic, parsley, lemon zest and juice, olive oil, and salt in a small bowl and mix well.

2. Gremolata will last about 5 days in the refrigerator, or several months frozen.

PER SERVING Calories: 426, Protein: 16g, Total Carbohydrates: 72g, Fiber: 3g, Total Fat: 9g, Saturated Fat: 1g, Cholesterol: 83mg, Sodium: 927mg

Pesto Pasta with Shrimp

Serves 4   Prep time: 15 minutes   Cook time: 10 to 15 minutes

QUICK & EASY   Talk about more bang for the buck! This is a very simple recipe of pasta, pesto, shrimp, and not much more. The pesto tints the pasta green, and the garlicky goodness works well with the sweetness of the shrimp. The first time I had this dish was at a very trendy Italian restaurant on Fisherman's Wharf in San Francisco, way, way back before anyone knew what pesto was in America. It opened worlds for me!

3 teaspoons salt, divided
1 pound linguini
½ cup Pesto (page 209)
1 pound cooked bay shrimp
¼ teaspoon red pepper flakes (optional)
2 tablespoons lemon juice
½ cup grated Parmesan cheese
Extra-virgin olive oil for drizzling

❋ I love the combination of shrimp and feta, so I often use crumbled feta instead of Parmesan cheese in this dish. If you can't find linguini, substitute fettuccini or spaghetti.

1. Fill a large pot with water and bring to a boil. Once boiling, add 2 teaspoons salt and cook the pasta according to the package directions.

2. Drain the pasta and put it back in the pot. Add the pesto, shrimp, 1 teaspoon salt, red pepper flakes (if using), and lemon juice, and mix well to combine.

3. Place in a serving dish. Top with Parmesan cheese and drizzle with olive oil before serving.

4. Leftovers can be stored in the refrigerator for 5 days or frozen for several months.

PER SERVING Calories: 617, Protein: 45g, Total Carbohydrates: 65g, Fiber: 1g, Total Fat: 20g, Saturated Fat: 5g, Cholesterol: 323mg, Sodium: 1772mg

Pasta with Smoked Salmon and Capers

Serves 4   Prep time: 15 minutes   Cook time: 10 to 15 minutes

QUICK & EASY   I love this dish hot, but if you make it with penne pasta or bowties it can be served cold as a great picnic salad. The creaminess of the yogurt is the perfect match for the smokiness of the salmon and the salty, sharp flavor of capers.

2½ teaspoons salt, divided

1 pound fettuccini

2 tablespoons extra-virgin olive oil, plus more for drizzling

1 cup plain Greek yogurt

3 scallions, thinly sliced

1 tablespoon lemon zest

1 tablespoon capers

¼ teaspoon freshly ground black pepper

8 ounces smoked salmon, cut into ¼-inch strips

1 tablespoon chopped fresh dill

❋ The smoked salmon is used as a garnish on top of the pasta, rather than mixed in. This is so the heat of the pasta doesn't cook the salmon, which changes its texture. Traditionally this pasta is made with mascarpone cheese; I've substituted Greek yogurt since it offers more protein and I like the tartness of yogurt in this dish.

1. Fill a large pot with water and bring to a boil. Once boiling, add 2 teaspoons salt and cook the pasta according to the package directions.

2. Drain the pasta and return it to the pot. Add the olive oil, yogurt, scallions, lemon zest, capers, ½ teaspoon salt, and the pepper, and mix well.

3. Place in a serving dish and arrange the smoked salmon over the top. Garnish with the dill and drizzle with olive oil before serving.

4. Leftovers can be stored in the refrigerator for 5 days. I do not recommend freezing smoked salmon.

PER SERVING Calories: 504, Protein: 27g, Total Carbohydrates: 68g, Fiber: 1g, Total Fat: 13g, Saturated Fat: 3g, Cholesterol: 100mg, Sodium: 1564mg

eight

Vegetarian & Vegan

Stuffed Tomatoes

Serves 4   Prep time: 20 minutes   Cook time: 30 minutes

VEGAN | GLUTEN-FREE | BIG 8 ALLERGEN-FRIENDLY   Stuffed vegetables were often on the table when I was growing up—mostly the result of an overabundance of a crop at the farm. This recipe uses tomatoes, but the same filling can be packed into bell peppers, large zucchini, or eggplant. This filling uses basmati rice, but other grains, such as barley or bulgur, would also work well.

4 large tomatoes
About 1½ cups water
1 cup basmati rice
1½ teaspoons salt, divided
2 tablespoons plus 1 teaspoon
    extra-virgin olive oil, divided
¼ cup chopped Kalamata olives
3 scallions, thinly sliced
1 garlic clove, minced
1 tablespoon lemon zest
1 tablespoon chopped fresh dill
¼ teaspoon freshly ground
    black pepper

❋ Instead of baking the tomatoes, you can serve this cold as a salad. Prep the tomatoes as described, cook the rice and let it cool to room temperature, add the remaining filling ingredients, and stuff the tomatoes. Drizzle with olive oil and a splash of vinegar, and serve.

1. Cut off the tops of the tomatoes, about ⅓ inch from the top at the stem end. These are the lids; set them aside.

2. Place a small strainer over a 2-cup measure cup. Using a spoon, remove the soft center and seeds from each tomato, allowing the liquid to drain into the measuring cup. Be sure to leave about a ¼-inch of tomato flesh in each tomato so it holds its shape. Let the scooped tomatoes drain upside down on a paper towel while preparing the rest of the recipe.

3. Top up the tomato liquid with water so you have 2 cups of liquid. Place the rice, tomato-water mixture, 1 teaspoon salt, and 1 teaspoon of olive oil in a medium saucepan and bring to a boil. Reduce to a simmer, cover, and cook 15 to 20 minutes, or until the rice is done.

4. Preheat the oven to 375°F. Oil an 8-by-8-inch baking sheet or an 8-inch pie plate.

5. Spoon the cooked rice into a medium bowl and add the olives, scallions, garlic, lemon zest, dill, ½ teaspoon salt, and pepper.

6. Gently fill each tomato with as much filling as you can get in without breaking the tomato.

7. Place the lids on the tomatoes and place them in the prepared pan. You may have filling left over.

8. Drizzle the remaining olive oil over the stuffed tomatoes and bake 15 minutes, until the tomatoes are wrinkled. Don't overbake or the tomatoes will break.

9. Let the tomatoes rest for 5 to 10 minutes before serving. This will make it easier to remove them from the baking dish.

10. Leftovers can be stored in the refrigerator for 2 or 3 days.

PER SERVING Calories: 289, Protein: 5g, Total Carbohydrates: 47g, Fiber: 4g, Total Fat: 10g, Saturated Fat: 1g, Cholesterol: 0mg, Sodium: 960mg

Rice with Fava Beans and Pistachios

Serves 4 to 6   Prep time: 10 minutes   Cook time: 20 minutes

QUICK & EASY | VEGAN | GLUTEN-FREE   This dish bursts with spring flavors. Rice pilaf creates the base for sautéed leeks, fava beans, and spring herbs. The buttery taste of pistachios adds a final crunch. Serve this dish with a crisp white wine.

1 cup basmati or other long-grain rice

4 tablespoons extra-virgin olive oil, divided

1 garlic clove, minced

1 teaspoon salt

2½ cups water or vegetable broth, divided

2 tablespoons lemon juice

2 leeks, root and top trimmed, thinly sliced

1 (10-ounce) package frozen fava beans, thawed

1 tablespoon chopped fresh chives

1 teaspoon chopped fresh tarragon

½ cup chopped unsalted pistachios

❋ Fava beans have a short season and require a lot of prep—first taking the beans from the pods, then removing the tough outer shell of each bean. Fortunately, many stores sell frozen fava beans in the frozen vegetable cases. If you can't find frozen fava beans in your market, substitute lima beans (and don't tell anyone!).

1. Place the rice, 1 tablespoon olive oil, garlic, salt, and 2 cups water or broth in a medium pot. Bring to a boil, reduce to a simmer, and cook, covered, for 15 to 20 minutes or until the rice is tender and all the water has evaporated. Add the lemon juice and stir.

2. Place 3 tablespoons of olive oil in a large skillet over high heat.

3. Add the leeks and sauté 5 to 7 minutes or until the leeks have lightly browned.

4. Add the fava beans and ½ cup water or broth and sauté an additional 3 to 5 minutes, or until the liquid has evaporated and the beans are tender.

5. Spoon the rice into a serving dish. Place the vegetables over the rice and top with the chives, tarragon, and pistachios.

6. Leftovers can be stored in the refrigerator for 3 or 4 days.

PER SERVING Calories: 601, Protein: 24g, Total Carbohydrates: 87g, Fiber: 20g, Total Fat: 19g, Saturated Fat: 3g, Cholesterol: 0mg, Sodium: 644mg

Lebanese Lentils and Rice with Caramelized Shallots

Serves 4 to 6   Prep time: 15 minutes   Cook time: 25 to 30 minutes

VEGAN | GLUTEN-FREE | BIG 8 ALLERGEN-FRIENDLY   This is my favorite dish to order at a Lebanese restaurant: fragrant rice and lentils topped with crispy fried onions. I've simplified this recipe by using canned lentils instead of dry, and I use shallots instead of onions because they quickly become crispy and golden brown when fried. I like the flavor of basmati rice, but any long-grain rice will work well.

½ cup plus 1 tablespoon extra-virgin olive oil, divided

¾ cup basmati rice

1 teaspoon whole cumin seeds

1 teaspoon salt

¼ teaspoon freshly ground black pepper

¼ teaspoon cayenne pepper

1 cinnamon stick

1½ cups water

1 (15-ounce) can lentils, drained and rinsed

2 large shallots, thinly sliced

½ lemon

✳ This is not a make-ahead dish, since the shallots will quickly lose their crunch. To tell if the oil is hot enough to fry the shallots, add one thin slice. If it bubbles in the oil, it's hot enough; if the shallot slice falls to the bottom of the pan, the oil is too cold.

1. Place 1 tablespoon olive oil in a medium pot over high heat.

2. Add the rice and cumin seeds and sauté until the rice is slightly toasted, about 5 minutes.

3. Add the salt, pepper, cayenne, cinnamon, and water. Cover and bring to a boil. Reduce to a simmer and cook, covered, for 15 to 20 minutes, or until the water is absorbed and the rice is tender.

4. Stir the lentils into the cooked rice.

5. Pour ½ cup olive oil into a frying pan over medium-high heat. When the oil is hot, add the shallots in batches and cook until crispy. Remove with a slotted spoon and drain on paper towels until all the shallots have been cooked.

6. Spoon the rice onto a serving platter, remove and discard the cinnamon stick, and top the dish with the shallots. Squeeze the lemon over all, and serve.

7. Leftovers can be stored in the refrigerator about 5 days.

PER SERVING Calories: 574, Protein: 15g, Total Carbohydrates: 58g, Fiber: 16g, Total Fat: 32g, Saturated Fat: 5g, Cholesterol: 0mg, Sodium: 587mg

Couscous with Roasted Vegetables

Serves 4 to 6   Prep time: 15 minutes   Cook time: 25 minutes

VEGAN   Couscous is not a grain–it's a pasta made from semolina flour shaped into little balls. Semolina is a type of wheat, but for many, it is more digestible than other flours made from wheat, because it has less gluten. Couscous is most famously eaten in Morocco, but it shows up in salads and main dishes throughout the Middle East and Africa. The good news is that it cooks in about 10 minutes.

3 cups peeled and seeded winter squash, cut into ½-inch cubes

10 Brussels sprouts, stemmed and cut in half

1 large red onion, cut into ½-inch dice

1 large red bell pepper, seeded and cut into ½-inch dice

1 garlic clove, minced

4 Roma tomatoes, each cut into 8 wedges

3 tablespoons extra-virgin olive oil, divided

1½ teaspoons salt, divided

¼ teaspoon cayenne pepper

3 cups water or vegetable broth

2 cups couscous

3 tablespoons golden raisins

¼ cup chopped fresh flatleaf parsley

✳ You can use any assortment of vegetables in this dish; it's perfect for finishing off summer's bounty. Toasted pine nuts are also a delicious addition. The vegetables can be prepped days ahead and warmed and added to the dish when you're ready to serve.

1. Preheat the oven to 400°F.

2. In a large bowl, combine the winter squash, Brussels sprouts, red onion, bell pepper, garlic, tomatoes, 2 tablespoons olive oil, 1 teaspoon salt, and cayenne pepper. Mix well.

3. Divide the vegetables among two rimmed baking sheets. Cover with foil and roast 10 minutes. Remove the foil and cook another 5 to 10 minutes, or until the vegetables are tender and slightly browned. Set aside.

4. Place the water or broth in a small saucepan and bring to a boil.

5. Place the couscous and raisins in a medium bowl. Pour the boiling water or broth over the couscous and raisins, cover the bowl, and let it sit for 10 minutes.

6. Remove the lid and fluff the couscous. Add ½ teaspoon salt, the parsley, and 1 tablespoon olive oil.

7. Mound the couscous onto a large serving platter. Using a spoon, push the couscous outward to build up a rim around the plate, creating a large space in the center of the couscous.

8. Spoon the roasted vegetables into the center and serve.

9. Leftovers can be stored in the refrigerator for 5 days or frozen a few months.

PER SERVING Calories: 571, Protein: 17g, Total Carbohydrates: 103g, Fiber: 15g, Total Fat: 12g, Saturated Fat: 2g, Cholesterol: 0mg, Sodium: 914mg

Mushroom Farro Risotto

Serves 4 to 6   Prep time: 15 minutes   Cook time: 20 to 25 minutes

VEGETARIAN   Farro replaces the more traditional arborio rice that is typically used in risotto. Farro is a variety of wheat that has been around in Italy so long, the ancient Romans ate it. It has more fiber and protein than rice. However, it does have gluten, so if you're sensitive, you may want to stick with rice.

2 tablespoons extra-virgin olive oil

1 large shallot, thinly sliced

10 large mushrooms, sliced

½ cup red wine

1 cup farro

1½ to 2 cups vegetable broth, warmed

½ cup Parmesan cheese

1 tablespoon chopped fresh
    flatleaf parsley

1 teaspoon salt

¼ teaspoon freshly ground
    black pepper

✻ To make this vegan, omit the cheese. Toasted walnuts are delicious in this dish.

1. Place a large skillet over high heat, add the olive oil and shallot, and sauté 3 to 5 minutes or until shallot is softened.

2. Add the mushrooms and red wine and simmer until the wine has evaporated.

3. Add the farro and sauté about 3 minutes to coat it with the flavors in the pan.

4. Add ½ cup broth and cook, stirring occasionally, until the broth has all been absorbed. Add an additional ½ cup broth and repeat. Continue until all the broth has been used and the farro is tender but not mushy, about 20 minutes.

5. Turn off the heat and add the Parmesan cheese, parsley, salt, and pepper. Serve immediately.

6. Leftovers will last about 1 week in the refrigerator.

PER SERVING Calories: 322, Protein: 14g, Total Carbohydrates: 38g, Fiber: 4g, Total Fat: 11g, Saturated Fat: 3g, Cholesterol: 10mg, Sodium: 924mg

Barley Pilaf with Roasted Beets and Pistachios

Serves 4 to 6   Prep time: 15 minutes   Cook time: 20 to 25 minutes

VEGAN   Barley is more than just a grain floating in soup! It is used frequently throughout the Mediterranean in a variety of ways, including ground into a flour to make bread. I like to make it into a classic pilaf and top it with roasted beets and pistachios, a beautiful and delicious combination. This recipe can be served room temperature as a salad instead of a hot dish.

4 tablespoons extra-virgin olive oil, divided
1 garlic clove, minced
1 cup barley
2 cups vegetable broth
1 teaspoon salt
¼ teaspoon freshly ground black pepper
4 large roasted beets, peeled and cut into eighths
1 tablespoon balsamic vinegar
¼ cup coarsely chopped unsalted pistachios
1 tablespoon chopped fresh dill

❋ To roast the beets, heat the oven to 400°F. Peel the beets, cut into eighths, and place them on a foil-lined baking sheet. Season the beets with salt and pepper and a drizzle of olive oil. Cover the beets with foil, creating a foil package, and roast them for 40 minutes or until tender. The beets can be made several days ahead and stored in the refrigerator.

1. Place a large skillet over high heat. Add 2 tablespoons olive oil, the garlic, and barley and sauté about 5 minutes to lightly toast the barley.

2. Add the broth, salt, and pepper and bring to a boil. Reduce to a simmer and cook 20 to 30 minutes, or until the barley is tender.

3. Mound the cooked barley onto a serving platter and arrange the roasted beets on top. Drizzle 2 tablespoons olive oil and the vinegar over the barley. Garnish with the pistachios and dill, and serve.

4. Leftovers can be stored in the refrigerator for about 4 days.

PER SERVING Calories: 359, Protein: 8g, Total Carbohydrates: 48g, Fiber: 11g, Total Fat: 17g, Saturated Fat: 2g, Cholesterol: 0mg, Sodium: 881mg

Eggplant and Bulgur Pilaf

Serves 4 to 6   Prep time: 40 minutes   Cook time: 25 minutes

VEGAN   Pilafs are a staple throughout the Middle East. The grain in the dish may be rice, wheat, or barley. This recipe is made with bulgur, a dried cracked wheat that doesn't have to be cooked. You simply soak the grain in boiling water until its soft and fluffy, which typically takes about 30 minutes.

1 cup bulgur

1 eggplant, peeled and cut into
    1-inch cubes

2 teaspoons salt, divided

4 tablespoons extra-virgin olive oil,
    divided

1 medium onion, diced

4 scallions, sliced

1 green bell pepper, seeded
    and chopped

1 large carrot, peeled and grated

2 garlic cloves, minced

2 tablespoons tomato paste

1 teaspoon dried oregano

¼ teaspoon ground cinnamon

½ cup chopped fresh flatleaf parsley

1 lemon, cut into wedges

✻ If you're making this with barley or rice, cook the grain first and proceed with the recipe as described above.

1. Place the bulgur in a large bowl and pour in enough boiling water to cover it by ½ inch. Cover and let it sit for 30 minutes.

2. Salt the eggplant cubes with 1 teaspoon salt and set aside for at least 10 minutes. Then dry the eggplant with paper towels.

3. Heat 3 tablespoons olive oil in a Dutch oven or a heavy pot with a lid over high heat.

4. Add the eggplant in a single layer and don't stir for the first 3 minutes, to brown it, then stir for an additional 5 minutes until softened.

5. Add the onion, scallions, bell pepper, carrot, and garlic, and sauté for 5 minutes.

6. Add the tomato paste, oregano, cinnamon, and 1 teaspoon salt, and cook 3 minutes.

7. Add the soaked bulgur and stir over low heat until well mixed. If the eggplant isn't soft enough, add ½ cup of water and cook until the water evaporates.

8. Add the remaining 1 tablespoon olive oil and the parsley. Serve with lemon wedges.

9. This dish will keep in the refrigerator for several days, or frozen for a few months.

PER SERVING Calories: 318, Protein: 7g, Total Carbohydrates: 44g, Fiber: 14g, Total Fat: 15g, Saturated Fat: 2g, Cholesterol: 0mg, Sodium: 910mg

Spinach Bourekas

Serves 6 to 8   Prep time: 20 minutes   Cook time: 20 to 25 minutes

VEGETARIAN   Bourekas are savory pastry turnovers. They can be made with phyllo or puff pastry, and can be filled with meats, cheeses, greens, or other vegetables. I've made this recipe super easy by making it one big pie instead of individual hand pies. Even vegetable haters love this pie. Puff pastry sheets are sold in the freezer section, typically next to the frozen pie shells.

2 teaspoons extra-virgin olive oil

2 sheets of puff pastry, thawed

1 (10-ounce) bag frozen chopped
    spinach, thawed, all liquid
    pressed out

1 small onion, diced

1 garlic clove, minced

2 eggs, beaten

2 ounces feta cheese, crumbled

1 teaspoon dried oregano

1 teaspoon salt

¼ teaspoon freshly ground
    black pepper

1 tablespoon sesame seeds

✳ If you want to make this with phyllo instead of puff pastry, you will need 8 sheets of phyllo. Brush a pie plate with olive oil. Stack the phyllo, brushing with olive oil in between each sheet. Lay the stack of oiled phyllo in the oiled pie plate, spoon in the filling, and fold the phyllo over the filling. Brush the top with olive oil, sprinkle with sesame seeds, and bake.

1. Preheat the oven to 375°F.

2. Brush a 9-inch ovenproof pie dish with olive oil.

3. Roll and trim one sheet of puff pastry on a lightly floured board until it is big enough to line the bottom of the pie dish with a 1 inch overhang for crimping. Set the lined dish aside.

4. Roll and trim the second sheet of pastry until it is big enough to fit as the top crust for the pie. Set aside.

5. In a medium bowl, combine the spinach, onion, and garlic. Add ¾ of the beaten eggs.

6. Mix the spinach mixture well and add the feta, oregano, salt, and pepper. Mix to combine.

7. Spoon the filling into the pastry-lined pie dish. Top with the top crust and crimp the edges to seal them.

8. Brush the top of the pastry with the remaining beaten egg and sprinkle with sesame seeds.

9. Bake 20 to 25 minutes or until the pastry is golden brown.

10. Allow to rest 5 to 10 minutes before serving.

11. The filling for bourekas can be made ahead and stored in the refrigerator, or the entire pie can be made ahead and kept frozen, unbaked, until you're ready to serve it. For best results, let the frozen pie thaw overnight in the refrigerator before baking.

PER SERVING Calories: 537, Protein: 11g, Total Carbohydrates: 41g, Fiber: 3g, Total Fat: 37g, Saturated Fat: 10g, Cholesterol: 63mg, Sodium: 756mg

Rice and Spinach Mold

Serves 4 to 6   Prep time: 15 minutes   Cook time: 50 minutes

VEGETARIAN | GLUTEN-FREE   Onions, rice, and spinach are cooked together here, packed into a mold, and baked. This dish looks far more complicated than it is, and is a good starting point for a buffet menu. I like to serve it with roasted vegetables and boiled artichokes.

1 tablespoon butter

3 tablespoons extra-virgin olive oil

1 medium white onion, diced

1¾ cups basmati or other long-grain white rice

1 (10-ounce) bag frozen chopped spinach, thawed, all liquid pressed out

1 teaspoon salt

¼ teaspoon freshly ground black pepper

3½ cups vegetable broth or water

½ cup chopped sun-dried tomatoes

1 tablespoon lemon zest

½ cup Parmesan cheese

2 eggs, beaten

❋ If you don't have a 1½-quart soufflé dish or metal bowl, you can make this in an 8-by-13-inch pan and serve it cut into squares. The success of this dish relies on how well you pack the rice into the mold, so press firmly when filling the mold.

1. Preheat the oven to 350°F.

2. Butter a 1½-quart soufflé dish or a 1½-quart metal bowl and set aside.

3. Place the olive oil and onion in a medium saucepan and sauté until the onions have slightly browned, about 7 minutes.

4. Add the rice, spinach, salt, pepper, and broth or water and bring to a boil. Reduce to a simmer and cook, covered, for 15 to 20 minutes, or until all the liquid is absorbed and the rice is tender.

5. Spoon the rice into a large bowl and fluff with a wooden spoon. Let it cool for 15 minutes.

6. Add the sun-dried tomatoes, lemon zest, Parmesan cheese, and eggs to the rice, and mix well.

7. Spoon the mixture into the buttered mold and press firmly. Smooth the top.

8. Cover the mold with a piece of foil and place it into a larger baking pan. Add boiling water to the larger pan, to reach halfway up the side of the mold. Bake 30 minutes.

9. Remove from the water and discard the foil. Place a serving dish over the mold and invert it onto the dish. Carefully remove the mold.

10. Serve cut into wedges.

11. Leftovers can be stored in the refrigerator for 5 days.

PER SERVING Calories: 534, Protein: 16g, Total Carbohydrates: 74g, Fiber: 4g, Total Fat: 20g, Saturated Fat: 6g, Cholesterol: 100mg, Sodium: 967mg

Tunisian Eggs with Peppers and Tomatoes

Serves 4   Prep time: 10 minutes   Cook time: 15 minutes

QUICK & EASY | VEGETARIAN | GLUTEN-FREE   A popular Tunisian dish, the eggs here are cooked in a thick sauce of tomatoes and peppers. Typically, the dish is made with harissa, which is a spicy red pepper and herb sauce or paste. It's available in specialty grocery stores and sometimes in the international section or the condiment aisle of the supermarket.

2 tablespoons extra-virgin olive oil

1 onion, thinly sliced

1 tablespoon paprika

1 teaspoon whole cumin seeds

1 garlic clove, minced

3 large tomatoes, cored and diced

1 large red bell pepper, seeded and chopped

1 large green bell pepper, seeded and chopped

1 tablespoon harissa

½ cup water or vegetable broth

1 teaspoon salt

4 eggs

2 tablespoons fresh flatleaf parsley, chopped

❋ If you can't find harissa but want to keep the heat, try 1 teaspoon chipotle powder or ½ teaspoon cayenne pepper. If you don't like spicy food, you can just omit it. A dollop of yogurt will help cool the spiciness of this dish.

1. Place the olive oil in a large skillet over high heat.

2. Add the onion, paprika, and cumin seeds and sauté 5 minutes to toast the spices.

3. Add the garlic, tomatoes, bell peppers, harissa, water or broth, and salt. Bring to a simmer and cook 5 to 7 minutes to thicken the sauce.

4. Using the back of a spoon, make four indentations in the sauce and carefully crack one egg into each indentation.

5. Cover the pan and cook 2 to 3 minutes to set the eggs.

6. Sprinkle the parsley over the cooked eggs and serve.

7. The sauce for this dish can be made ahead and stored in the fridge for 1 week or the freezer for several months.

PER SERVING Calories: 205, Protein: 9g, Total Carbohydrates: 16g, Fiber: 5g, Total Fat: 13g, Saturated Fat: 3g, Cholesterol: 165mg, Sodium: 703mg

Egyptian Spinach Omelet

Serves 4   Prep time: 10 minutes   Cook time: 20 minutes

QUICK & EASY | VEGETARIAN | GLUTEN-FREE   I know this is called an Egyptian omelet, but it was a standard supper in my house. It typically showed up on the table when tomatoes were in season. Instead of flipping the omelet, I finish it in a hot oven.

3 tablespoons extra-virgin olive oil

1 small onion, chopped

1 garlic clove, minced

3 cups spinach, firmly packed

4 large ripe tomatoes, cored and chopped

1 teaspoon salt

¼ teaspoon freshly ground black pepper

8 eggs, beaten

2 ounces feta cheese, crumbled

1 tablespoon chopped fresh flatleaf parsley

✳ The onions and tomatoes can be prepped ahead and kept in the refrigerator until you are ready to make the omelet. Basil, mint, and oregano all work well in this recipe.

1. Preheat the oven to 400°F.

2. Put olive oil in a large ovenproof skillet over high heat. Add the onions and sauté 5 to 7 minutes, or until the onions have softened.

3. Add the spinach, garlic, tomatoes, salt, and pepper and simmer another 5 minutes, until most of the liquid has evaporated.

4. Pour the beaten eggs into the spinach and tomato mixture and mix slightly, then leave the eggs undisturbed for 3 to 5 minutes, or until they have set on the bottom.

5. Place the pan in the oven and bake an additional 5 minutes, or until the eggs are just set.

6. Remove from the oven and top with feta and parsley. Cut into wedges and serve.

7. Leftovers will keep in the refrigerator for 3 or 4 days.

PER SERVING Calories: 300, Protein: 16g, Total Carbohydrates: 11g, Fiber: 3g, Total Fat: 23g, Saturated Fat: 5g, Cholesterol: 340mg, Sodium: 891mg

Potato, Leek, and Mushroom Patties

Serves 4   Prep time: 40 minutes   Cook time: 20 minutes

VEGAN | GLUTEN-FREE | BIG 8 ALLERGEN-FRIENDLY   This is a good way to use leftover mashed potatoes. In this recipe they are mixed with sautéed leeks and mushrooms, shaped into patties, and pan fried. The leeks and mushrooms make them irresistible. This is perfect for Sunday supper. Add Lemon Almond Soup (page 78) for a light French meal.

4 medium russet potatoes, peeled and cut into 1-inch dice

1 teaspoon salt

¼ teaspoon freshly ground black pepper

⅛ teaspoon ground nutmeg

½ cup plus 2 tablespoons extra-virgin olive oil, divided, plus more to oil the pan

1 leek, root and top trimmed, thinly sliced

4 ounces mushrooms, thinly sliced

1 garlic clove, thinly sliced

¼ cup white wine

❊ The success of this dish depends on making sure the potatoes are as dry as can be before mashing. Once drained, if the potatoes still look wet, return them to the pot and place over low heat for several minutes to dry them. Parmesan cheese is a delicious addition to this recipe; just add some to the mashed potatoes.

1. Place the potatoes in a large pot, cover with water, and bring to a boil. Cook until the potatoes are tender, about 10 to 15 minutes.

2. Drain the potatoes and mash with the salt, pepper, and nutmeg. Set aside.

3. In a large skillet, add 2 tablespoons olive oil and the leek and sauté over high heat for 3 minutes, until softened. Add the mushrooms, garlic, and wine and cook until all the liquid has evaporated, about 10 minutes.

4. Add the cooked vegetables to the mashed potatoes and mix well. Let the mixture sit at least 30 minutes before shaping the patties.

5. Place the remaining ½ cup olive oil in a medium skillet over medium-high heat.

6. Scoop up about ½ cup of the potato mixture and shape into a patty. Place the patty in the hot olive oil and cook until golden, about 3 minutes. Turn the patty and brown the other side.

7. Place the cooked patties on a serving platter and keep them warm until all the patties are cooked. This recipe makes about 8 to 10 patties.

8. These patties can be made ahead and stored in the refrigerator until you're ready to cook, or they can be fried and stored at room temperature for several hours, to be reheated in the oven when you're ready to serve.

PER SERVING Calories: 480, Protein: 5g, Total Carbohydrates: 38g, Fiber: 6g, Total Fat: 35g, Saturated Fat: 5g, Cholesterol: 0mg, Sodium: 601mg

Layered Vegetable Casserole

Serves 8   Prep time: 30 minutes   Cook time: 35 to 45 minutes

VEGETARIAN | GLUTEN-FREE   Think of this as a pasta-free lasagna. Roasted vegetables are layered with pesto-laced ricotta and topped with mozzarella. Eggplant and zucchini are used in this recipe, but in the winter, substitute slices of winter squash and mushrooms for a seasonal casserole.

3 tablespoons extra-virgin olive oil, plus more to oil the pan

1 large eggplant, cut into ¼-inch slices

3 large zucchini, cut lengthwise into ¼-inch slices

2 teaspoons salt, divided

2 bell peppers (any color), seeded and cut into wide strips

¼ teaspoon freshly ground black pepper

1 pound ricotta cheese

½ cup Pesto (page 209)

½ cup Parmesan cheese

2 scallions, thinly sliced

1 pound mozzarella cheese, sliced or shredded

❋ This is a perfect make-ahead dish. You can assemble it several days ahead and bake it before serving. For best results, allow the casserole to come to room temperature before baking.

1. Preheat the oven to 400°F.

2. Oil a 9-by-13-inch pan.

3. Place the eggplant and zucchini in a single layer on a work surface or baking sheet, sprinkle with 1 teaspoon salt, and let them sit for 15 minutes. Pat the vegetables dry with a paper towel.

4. In a large bowl, combine the eggplant, zucchini, bell peppers, olive oil, 1 teaspoon salt, and pepper. Mix to coat the vegetables, being careful not to break them.

5. Lay the vegetables in a single layer on baking sheets and place in the oven.

6. Roast the vegetables until lightly browned on one side, about 7 to 10 minutes. Remove from the oven, turn the vegetables over, and return to the oven to brown the other side.

7. While the vegetables are roasting, in a medium bowl combine the ricotta, pesto, Parmesan cheese, and scallions. ➹

8. Place a layer of roasted vegetables in the oiled pan. Top with half the ricotta mixture and ⅓ of the mozzarella. Top with another layer of vegetables, then the remaining ricotta mixture and ⅓ of the mozzarella. Finish with one last layer of vegetables and spread the remaining mozzarella over the top layer of vegetables. You'll have three layers of vegetables and two layers of filling in all.

9. Reduce the oven to 375°F. Cover the casserole with foil and bake 20 minutes. Remove the foil and continue to bake until the cheese is bubbly and lightly browned.

10. Let the casserole sit about 15 minutes before serving.

11. Once baked, the casserole can be cut into single-serving portions and frozen for several months.

PER SERVING Calories: 420, Protein: 29g, Total Carbohydrates: 16g, Fiber: 4g, Total Fat: 28g, Saturated Fat: 12g, Cholesterol: 57mg, Sodium: 882mg

Minestrone

Serves 6 to 8   Prep time: 15 minutes   Cook time: 20 minutes

QUICK & EASY | VEGETARIAN   A minestrone is a tomato-based broth loaded with anything you can think of. Typically there is zucchini and beans in it, along with pasta. But you really can add whatever you'd like, whatever is in season, including bits and pieces of leftover vegetables and meats. It's a nourishing way to use what you have.

¼ cup extra-virgin olive oil

1 onion, thinly diced

2 garlic cloves, minced

2 celery stalks, chopped

1 large carrot, peeled and chopped

1½ cups green beans (fresh or frozen), cut into ½-inch pieces

1 teaspoon dried oregano

1 teaspoon dried basil

1 teaspoon salt

¼ teaspoon freshly ground black pepper

1 (28-ounce) can crushed tomatoes

4 cups chicken or vegetable broth

1 cup elbow, small shell, or other small pasta

½ cup grated Parmesan cheese

3 tablespoons chopped fresh basil

✳ You can make this soup gluten-free by omitting the pasta or using gluten-free pasta.

1. Heat the olive oil in a large Dutch oven or a heavy pot with a lid.

2. Add the onion and sauté until it is lightly browned.

3. Add garlic, celery, carrot, green beans, oregano, basil, salt, and pepper, and sauté for 5 minutes.

4. Add the crushed tomatoes, broth, and pasta, and bring to a boil. Cook 5 to 7 minutes or until pasta is done.

5. Ladle soup into bowls and serve with Parmesan cheese and chopped fresh basil on top.

6. This soup will taste better the next day and will last in the refrigerator for about 1 week and in the freezer for longer. If you're making it ahead, add the Parmesan cheese and fresh basil right before serving.

PER SERVING Calories: 251, Protein: 11g, Total Carbohydrates: 29g, Fiber: 6g, Total Fat: 11g, Saturated Fat: 3g, Cholesterol: 22mg, Sodium: 797mg

Hearty Tuscan Vegetable Stew

Serves 4 to 6   Prep time: 15 minutes   Cook time: 15 minutes

QUICK & EASY | VEGAN   While this is technically a soup, it's so thick you can call it stew. This recipe is loaded with vegetables and legumes–the classic Mediterranean diet. I like to serve this with a grilled or toasted hearty bread that I've brushed with olive oil and crushed garlic, with a sprinkling of dried Italian seasonings, and a handful of Parmesan cheese atop the stew.

3 tablespoons extra-virgin olive oil

1 onion, chopped

2 garlic cloves, chopped

2 zucchini, chopped

1 bell pepper (any color), seeded and chopped

2 large tomatoes, chopped

1 carrot, peeled and chopped

4 cups vegetable broth

1 teaspoon salt

½ teaspoon freshly ground black pepper

½ teaspoon dried rosemary

1 (15.5-ounce) can white beans, drained and rinsed

1 (15.5-ounce) can black beans, drained and rinsed

½ cup chopped fresh flatleaf parsley

❋ I chose summer vegetables for this recipe, but you can substitute winter vegetables (squashes and root vegetables) instead. You can also make this in a slow cooker. Place everything but the beans and parsley in a slow cooker and cook on high for 2 hours. Stir in the beans and parsley, and serve.

1. Place a Dutch oven or a heavy pot with a lid over high heat. Add the olive oil, onion, and garlic and sauté 3 to 5 minutes, or until the onions have softened.

2. Add the zucchini, bell pepper, tomatoes, and carrot and sauté an additional 3 minutes.

3. Add the broth, salt, pepper, and rosemary and bring to a boil. Reduce to a simmer and cook 5 minutes.

4. Add the beans and cook an additional minute or two to heat the beans through.

5. Ladle into bowls and garnish with chopped parsley.

6. This soup can be stored in the refrigerator for 5 days and frozen for several months.

PER SERVING Calories: 504, Protein: 26g, Total Carbohydrates: 79g, Fiber: 19g, Total Fat: 13g, Saturated Fat: 2g, Cholesterol: 0mg, Sodium: 1013mg

Winter Squash Stew

Serves 4 to 6   Prep time: 15 minutes   Cook time: 4 hours

VEGAN | GLUTEN-FREE | BIG 8 ALLERGEN-FRIENDLY   I love this recipe! Throw everything in a slow cooker, forget about it for 4 hours, and it's done. I like to ladle this over bowls of rice and dollop it with Greek yogurt and Gremolata (page 119).

3 tablespoons extra-virgin olive oil

1 pound butternut squash, peeled, seeded, and cut into 1-inch cubes

1 medium onion, thinly sliced

2 garlic cloves, sliced

2 tablespoons tomato paste

1 (15-ounce) can garbanzo beans, drained and rinsed

1 teaspoon salt

1 teaspoon paprika

¼ teaspoon red pepper flakes (optional)

4 cups water or vegetable broth

½ teaspoon dried rosemary

1 bunch Swiss chard, washed and chopped

✳ Any winter squash will work in this recipe, but kabocha and butternut squash make a really delicious combination.

1. Place the olive oil, squash, onion, garlic, tomato paste, garbanzo beans, salt, paprika, red pepper flakes (if using), water or vegetable broth, and rosemary in a slow cooker. Stir to mix.

2. Cover and cook on high for 4 hours.

3. Add the Swiss chard and stir to wilt.

4. This stew can be stored in the refrigerator for 1 week or frozen for months.

PER SERVING Calories: 310, Protein: 8g, Total Carbohydrates: 44g, Fiber: 8g, Total Fat: 12g, Saturated Fat: 2g, Cholesterol: 0mg, Sodium: 988mg

nine

Fish & Seafood

Swordfish Souvlaki with Oregano

Serves 4   Prep time: 15 minutes   Cook time: 15 minutes

QUICK & EASY | GLUTEN-FREE   The firm texture and unique flavor of swordfish make it perfect for skewering and grilling. I love the flavor of lemon and oregano with the little bits of charred swordfish. Tuna and halibut also work well on a skewer. Serve this with rice and Greek Village Salad (page 84) for a classic Mediterranean meal.

1½ pounds swordfish, cut into
    1½-inch cubes
1 pint cherry tomatoes
¼ cup extra-virgin olive oil
¼ cup lemon juice
1½ teaspoons dried oregano
1 teaspoon salt
¼ teaspoon freshly ground
    black pepper
8 skewers
Lemon wedges for garnish

❋ The fish can marinate, covered, for several hours in the refrigerator. Leave out the tomatoes, and add them 15 minutes before you make the skewers. In general, it's best not to refrigerate tomatoes, if you can help it, since they lose flavor and texture when chilled.

1. Place the swordfish and cherry tomatoes in a large bowl.

2. Add the olive oil, lemon juice, oregano, salt, and pepper, and mix well.

3. Let it sit for at least 15 minutes before skewering, so the flavors can blend.

4. Thread the swordfish and tomatoes onto the skewers.

5. Heat the grill until hot or use a stovetop grill pan.

6. Grill each skewer 3 to 5 minutes per side, until the fish is lightly browned and cooked through.

7. Arrange the skewers on a platter, garnish with lemon wedges, and serve.

8. Once cooked, the fish should be eaten within 2 days.

PER SERVING Calories: 394, Protein: 44g, Total Carbohydrates: 4g, Fiber: 1g, Total Fat: 22g, Saturated Fat: 4g, Cholesterol: 85mg, Sodium: 785mg

Pistachio-Crusted Salmon

Serves 4   Prep time: 15 minutes   Cook time: 15 minutes

QUICK & EASY | GLUTEN-FREE   This is the kind of fish dish that even people who don't like fish will like. Salmon's rich flavor is perfectly paired with the buttery taste of pistachios. This dish is beautiful, which makes it perfect for entertaining. Serve with asparagus and grilled pita bread for a dinner that looks like it took a lot more effort than it did.

1 tablespoon extra-virgin olive oil

1½ pounds salmon fillets

4 tablespoons Dijon mustard

¾ cup unsalted pistachios, coarsely chopped

1 tablespoon chopped fresh chives

1 teaspoon chopped fresh tarragon

1 garlic clove, minced

1 teaspoon salt

½ cup white wine

Lemon wedges for garnish

✳ Cod or tuna can replace the salmon in this recipe. The nut mixture can be made ahead and stored in the refrigerator for several days.

1. Preheat the oven to 400°F.

2. Brush a rimmed baking sheet with olive oil. Place the salmon fillets skin side down on the oiled baking sheet. Brush each fillet with mustard.

3. In a small bowl, combine the pistachios, chives, tarragon, garlic, and salt.

4. Press the nut mixture into the mustard on each fillet.

5. Carefully pour the wine into the pan, being careful not to rinse off the pistachio topping.

6. Bake for 15 to 20 minutes, or until the fish is firm.

7. Let rest for 5 minutes before serving with lemon wedges.

8. Once baked, the salmon can be stored in the refrigerator for 4 days.

PER SERVING Calories: 352, Protein: 36g, Total Carbohydrates: 5g, Fiber: 2g, Total Fat: 20g, Saturated Fat: 3g, Cholesterol: 75mg, Sodium: 895mg

Tilapia with Fresh Pesto

Good

Serves 4   Prep time: 15 minutes   Cook time: 10 minutes

QUICK & EASY | GLUTEN-FREE   Tilapia is a mild-flavored freshwater white fish that is easily found in most markets. It is an ancient fish that is eaten throughout the Middle East. Tilapia fillets are thin, so they cook quickly. The fresh pesto is made with spinach and basil, sneaking a serving of greens into dinner.

FOR THE PESTO

2 cups firmly packed baby spinach
6 large fresh basil leaves
1 garlic clove, coarsely chopped
¼ cup extra-virgin olive oil
1 teaspoon salt
¼ teaspoon freshly ground
    black pepper
1 tablespoon lemon zest

FOR THE TILAPIA

2 tablespoons extra-virgin olive oil
¾ cup rice flour
1 teaspoon salt
1 teaspoon paprika
1½ pounds tilapia fillets
Lemon wedges for garnish

✻ Using rice flour makes this dish gluten-free, but all-purpose flour will work as well. This recipe works well with any firm-fleshed white fish.

MAKE THE PESTO

1. Combine the baby spinach, basil, garlic, olive oil, salt, pepper, and lemon zest in a blender or food processor and process until smooth.

2. Set aside for the flavors to blend.

3. The pesto will stay fresh for 4 days in the refrigerator, and several months in the freezer.

MAKE THE TILAPIA

1. Preheat the oven to 400°F.

2. Place the olive oil in a 9-by-13-inch roasting pan and swirl to coat the pan. Set aside.

3. Combine the rice flour, salt, and paprika in a shallow dish.

4. Press each tilapia fillet into the rice flour mixture to coat on both sides. Set in the prepared roasting pan.

5. When all the fillets have been coated, bake 10 to 15 minutes or until the fish is firm to the touch.

6. Arrange the fillets on a serving platter and spoon the pesto over top. Serve with lemon wedges.

7. The fish should be eaten within 2 days of cooking it.

PER SERVING Calories: 424, Protein: 34g, Total Carbohydrates: 25g, Fiber: 1g, Total Fat: 22g, Saturated Fat: 4g, Cholesterol: 83mg, Sodium: 1235mg

Grilled Tuna with Romanesco Sauce

Serves 4   Prep time: 15 minutes   Cook time: 15 minutes

QUICK & EASY   Tuna steaks are perfect for grilling because they are firm-fleshed and have enough natural fat to stay moist despite the high heat. Tuna is expensive, but this dish is so amazing it's worth the occasional splurge. Romanesco sauce is a classic Spanish red pepper almond sauce that has many uses. It can be stirred into paella, spooned over steak, or combined with mayonnaise and served as a dip for vegetables.

FOR THE ROMANESCO SAUCE
⅓ cup extra-virgin olive oil
1 slice white bread, crusts removed
3 garlic cloves, crushed
¾ cup blanched (skinless) unsalted almonds
1 tablespoon lemon juice
1 teaspoon salt
½ teaspoon paprika
1 (12-ounce) jar roasted red peppers, drained
1 (14.5-ounce) can fire-roasted tomatoes

FOR THE TUNA
4 (6-ounce) tuna steaks
Extra-virgin olive oil
1 teaspoon salt
¼ teaspoon freshly ground black pepper
Lemon wedges for serving

✼ You can use swordfish or salmon in this recipe instead of tuna.

MAKE THE ROMANESCO SAUCE

1. Warm the olive oil in a medium skillet. Add the slice of bread and toast until brown.

2. Add the garlic to the pan and cook 1 minute more.

3. Place the fried bread and garlic, almonds, lemon juice, salt, paprika, roasted peppers, and tomatoes in a food processor or blender and process until the sauce is smooth and thick, with a bit of texture.

4. Romanesco sauce can be made ahead and stored in the refrigerator for several weeks, or can be frozen for several months.

MAKE THE TUNA

1. Heat a grill or stovetop grill until hot.

2. Rub the tuna steaks with olive oil and sprinkle with the salt and pepper.

3. Grill the steaks until they are golden on both sides, about 3 to 4 minutes per side.

4. Remove the steaks and let rest for 5 minutes before serving.

5. To serve, arrange the tuna on a serving platter and spoon the sauce over the top, and garnish with lemon wedges.

6. The grilled tuna will last 4 days in the refrigerator.

PER SERVING Calories: 611, Protein: 57g, Total Carbohydrates: 15g, Fiber: 5g, Total Fat: 37g, Saturated Fat: 6g, Cholesterol: 83mg, Sodium: 1089mg

Baked Cod with Tomatoes, Olives, and Preserved Lemons

Serves 4   Prep time: 15 minutes   Cook time: 15 minutes, plus 1 day for the lemons to cure

QUICK & EASY | GLUTEN-FREE   Cod is a wonderfully versatile fish. It is often packed in salt and dried to preserve it, and then reconstituted and used in many dishes throughout Europe and the Middle East. This recipe is made with fresh cod, which is faster to work with. Preserved lemons are lemons packed in salt and allowed to cure. You use them whole, with the skin. I've provided a quick version of preserved lemons, or you can find them at Greek or Middle Eastern markets. If you don't have them on hand, just sprinkle lemon zest over the dish before serving. It will still be delicious.

FOR THE QUICK PRESERVED LEMONS

3 lemons, scrubbed and cut into
   6 wedges each

⅓ cup lemon juice

3 tablespoons kosher salt

FOR THE COD

2 tablespoons extra-virgin olive oil

1 fennel bulb, thinly sliced

1 small red onion, thinly sliced

6 Roma tomatoes, cut into quarters

½ cup red wine

1½ pounds fresh cod fillets

1 teaspoon salt

¼ teaspoon freshly ground
   black pepper

½ cup pitted green olives

¼ cup chopped preserved lemons
   (or 1 tablespoon lemon zest)

1 tablespoon chopped fresh dill

❋ The fennel, onions, and tomatoes can be roasted ahead and stored in the refrigerator until you're ready to bake the cod.

MAKE THE QUICK PRESERVED LEMONS

1. Preheat the oven to 350°F.

2. Place the lemon wedges on a baking sheet and bake for 15 minutes.

3. Place the warm wedges in a large canning jar and add the lemon juice and kosher salt.

4. Seal tightly and shake to combine the ingredients.

5. Store in the refrigerator for at least 24 hours before using.

6. Preserved lemons will last several months in the refrigerator.

MAKE THE COD

1. Preheat the oven to 375°F.

2. Place the olive oil, fennel, onion, tomato, and wine in a 9-by-13-inch baking dish. Roast for 15 minutes to soften the vegetables.

3. While the vegetables are cooking, season the cod with salt and pepper.

4. Place the cod over the roasted vegetables. Cover with foil and bake 15 minutes, or until the cod is firm.

5. Remove from the oven. Add the olives, preserved lemons, and dill and serve.

6. Once cooked, the dish should be eaten within 3 days, or it can be frozen for 1 month.

PER SERVING Calories: 355, Protein: 42g, Total Carbohydrates: 17g, Fiber: 6g, Total Fat: 12g, Saturated Fat: 2g, Cholesterol: 94mg, Sodium: 1094mg

Halibut Baked in White Wine with Salsa Verde

Serves 4   Prep time: 15 minutes   Cook time: 15 minutes

QUICK & EASY | GLUTEN-FREE   Halibut was a splurge in my household growing up. It wasn't always available, and was a bit out of our price range, but I love it. It has a very delicate flavor, but it also has body and a buttery finish that pairs really well with the Salsa Verde.

FOR THE SALSA VERDE

2 bunches flatleaf parsley,
    stems removed
½ cup pine nuts (pignoli)
5 small gherkins
8 pitted green olives
3 garlic cloves, crushed
3 tablespoons white wine vinegar
1 teaspoon salt
¼ teaspoon freshly ground
    black pepper
1 cup extra-virgin olive oil

FOR THE HALIBUT

⅔ cup white wine
½ cup water
2 bay leaves
2 sprigs fresh flatleaf parsley
1 teaspoon salt
¼ teaspoon freshly ground
    black pepper
Several saffron threads (optional)
4 halibut steaks

✻ This dish can be eaten warm or cold. Warm, it's delicious with roasted potatoes and Turkish Bean Salad (page 63), or cold, served over a bed of greens with Moroccan Carrot Salad with Cinnamon (page 62).

MAKE THE SALSA VERDE

1. Place all ingredients except the olive oil in a food processor or blender and pulse until finely chopped.

2. With the machine running, gradually pour in the olive oil in a thin stream.

3. After all the olive oil has been added, store the sauce in a jar in the refrigerator.

4. The salsa verde can be made ahead and stored in the refrigerator for several weeks, or can be frozen for several months.

MAKE THE HALIBUT

1. Preheat the oven to 375°F.

2. Place the wine, water, bay leaves, parsley, salt, pepper, and saffron (if using) in a 9-by-13-inch baking dish.

3. Place the halibut steaks in the pan and cover with foil. Bake 15 to 20 minutes or until the fish is firm.

4. Remove from the oven and let rest 5 minutes in the pan.

5. To serve, remove the fish with a slotted spoon, arrange on a platter, discard the bay leaves and parsley sprigs, and spoon the sauce over the fish.

6. The baked halibut will keep 4 days in the refrigerator.

PER SERVING Calories: 574, Protein: 47g, Total Carbohydrates: 7g, Fiber: 1g, Total Fat: 37g, Saturated Fat: 5g, Cholesterol: 70mg, Sodium: 1183mg

Fish Couscous

Serves 4   Prep time: 10 minutes   Cook time: 20 minutes

QUICK & EASY   Most couscous dishes have a touch of sweetness to them; this recipe uses raisins, but fresh grapes will also be delicious if they are in season. A firm-fleshed white fish is best in this dish, such as cod or whiting. The fish is cooked in a garlic-ginger sauce and is spooned over the couscous and finished with toasted pine nuts.

1 cup couscous

2 teaspoons salt, divided

4 tablespoons extra-virgin olive oil, divided

1 cinnamon stick

2 cloves garlic, minced

1 (½-inch) slice fresh ginger, peeled and minced

1 (28-ounce) can fire-roasted tomatoes

½ cup golden raisins

2 teaspoons sugar or honey

1 small serrano chile, seeded and minced

1 pound white fish fillets

1 tablespoon lemon juice

¼ cup toasted pine nuts (pignoli)

1 tablespoon chopped fresh cilantro

✳ If you're avoiding wheat, you can make this dish with cooked rice as the base instead of couscous.

1. Place the couscous, 1 teaspoon salt, 2 tablespoons olive oil, and the cinnamon stick in a medium bowl. Add enough hot water to cover the couscous by ½ inch. Cover and let it sit for 30 minutes, until the couscous has absorbed the water.

2. Place a large skillet over high heat. Add the remaining 2 tablespoons olive oil and the garlic and sauté about 1 minute, until the garlic begins to brown.

3. Add the ginger, tomatoes, raisins, sugar or honey, 1 teaspoon salt, and chile and simmer 5 minutes.

4. Gently slide the fish into the tomato sauce and simmer, covered, 5 minutes more.

5. Add the lemon juice to the fish sauce.

6. Remove the cinnamon stick from the couscous, fluff with a fork, and mound onto a platter. Push the couscous to the edges of the dish to create a well.

7. Spoon the fish and sauce into the well. Garnish with toasted pine nuts and cilantro.

8. This dish can be stored in the refrigerator for 3 days. The couscous doesn't freeze well.

PER SERVING Calories: 636, Protein: 37g, Total Carbohydrates: 59g, Fiber: 6g, Total Fat: 29g, Saturated Fat: 4g, Cholesterol: 87mg, Sodium: 1254mg

Fish Paella

Serves 4 to 6   Prep time: 10 minutes   Cook time: 20 minutes

QUICK & EASY | GLUTEN-FREE   Paella is the quintessential one-pot meal. In Spain, paella is a national dish; it's available everywhere, and varies from city to city, depending on the local ingredients and traditions. Paella can have poultry, meats, or seafood in it. Some regions have seafood only. It is often served with Romanesco Sauce (page 147). The pepper and almond sauce is the perfect condiment for this fish paella.

¼ cup extra-virgin olive oil
1 Spanish onion, chopped
1 fennel bulb, chopped
1 red or yellow bell pepper, seeded
     and sliced into thin strips
1 clove garlic, minced
1 cup basmati or other long-grain rice
1½ cups chicken broth or water
½ cup white wine
1 teaspoon salt
¼ teaspoon freshly ground
     black pepper
¼ teaspoon saffron threads
½ pound salmon fillet, cut into
     1-inch cubes
½ pound cod or other white fish,
     cut into 1-inch cubes
1 cup frozen peas, thawed
¼ cup chopped fresh flatleaf parsley
1 recipe Romanesco Sauce (page 147)

❋ Any seafood or shellfish can be used in this dish. You can also add some cooked chicken or cooked sausage.

1. Place a large frying pan over high heat. Add the olive oil, onion, and fennel and sauté 2 minutes to soften the vegetables.

2. Add the bell peppers and garlic and sauté an additional 2 minutes.

3. Add the rice and mix well to coat the rice with the juices in the pan.

4. Add the chicken broth or water, wine, salt, pepper, and saffron. Bring to a boil. Reduce to a simmer, cover, and simmer 10 minutes.

5. Add the fish, cover, and cook an additional 5 minutes or until the rice is tender and the fish is cooked through.

6. Garnish with peas and parsley, and serve with Romanesco Sauce on the side.

7. Cooked paella can be stored for 4 days in the refrigerator.

PER SERVING Calories: 844, Protein: 38g, Total Carbohydrates: 68g, Fiber: 11g, Total Fat: 47g, Saturated Fat: 6g, Cholesterol: 69mg, Sodium: 1516mg

Tunisian Fish Soup with Potatoes

Serves 4   Prep time: 10 minutes   Cook time: 20 minutes

QUICK & EASY | GLUTEN FREE   Potatoes and fish are simmered in tomato broth aromatic with cumin and paprika. There are two types of paprika commonly used in Europe and the Middle East. One is called *sweet paprika* and the other is called *hot paprika*. This recipe calls for hot paprika (which is not all that hot, really), but you can use sweet if you don't like spicy. If you can't find hot paprika in your market, chipotle powder makes a good substitute.

2 large potatoes, peeled and cut
    into ½-inch cubes
3 Roma tomatoes, diced
3 tablespoons extra-virgin olive oil
1 teaspoon hot paprika
½ teaspoon ground cumin
2 cloves garlic, minced
1 teaspoon salt
4 cups water or chicken broth
1 pound white fish fillets
2 tablespoons lemon juice
¼ cup chopped fresh cilantro

❄ Any firm-fleshed white fish or shellfish works in this recipe. Buy what's freshest in the market.

1. Place the potatoes, tomatoes, olive oil, paprika, cumin, garlic, salt, and water or broth in a large Dutch oven or a heavy pot with a lid. Bring to a boil. Reduce to a simmer and cook until the potatoes are tender, about 10 to 15 minutes.

2. Slide the fish into the broth and cook an additional 5 minutes.

3. Add the lemon juice and cilantro, and serve.

4. The base for the soup, without the fish, can be made ahead and stored in the refrigerator for 1 week or in the freezer for several months. Once the fish has been added, it should be eaten within 3 days.

PER SERVING Calories: 434, Protein: 32g, Total Carbohydrates: 33g, Fiber: 6g, Total Fat: 20g, Saturated Fat: 3g, Cholesterol: 87mg, Sodium: 1455mg

Fish Stew with Roasted Red Pepper Sauce

Serves 4   Prep time: 15 minutes   Cook time: 15 minutes

QUICK & EASY | GLUTEN-FREE   A Tunisian pepper and tomato sauce makes the base for this stew, and the flavors are so versatile that you can use any type of fish or shellfish for this recipe. I like to add a few threads of saffron to this dish for color and flavor, but it can be omitted. It's a hearty stew, so serve it over a thick slice of toasted country bread to soak up all the sauce.

2 tablespoons extra-virgin olive oil, plus more to drizzle

2 teaspoons paprika

½ teaspoon ground cumin

Several saffron threads (optional)

1 onion, chopped

1 garlic clove, minced

4 Roma tomatoes, cored and diced.

2 large red bell peppers, roasted, peeled, seeded, and chopped

½ cup water or chicken broth

1 teaspoon salt

1½ pounds firm-flesh fish, cut into 1-inch cubes

2 tablespoons fresh flatleaf parsley, chopped

✽ To roast peppers, place whole peppers over a flame on the grill or stovetop and let char on all sides. Place in a paper bag to "sweat" for 5 to 10 minutes. Scrape off the charred flesh with a knife.

1. Place a Dutch oven or a heavy pot with a lid over high heat. Add the olive oil, paprika, cumin, saffron (if using), onion, and garlic. Sauté for 5 minutes to soften the vegetables. Add the tomatoes, roasted peppers, water or broth, and salt, and simmer 10 minutes.

2. Pour the vegetables into a blender or food processor and process until smooth. Return the sauce to the pot and bring to a simmer.

3. Gently add the fish to the sauce, cover, and cook 5 minutes.

4. Ladle into bowls, drizzle with olive oil, garnish with parsley, and serve.

5. The sauce (without the fish) can be made ahead and stored in the refrigerator for 1 week, or frozen for several months. Once the stew has been made, it's best to eat it within 3 days or freeze it for 1 month.

PER SERVING Calories: 349, Protein: 36g, Total Carbohydrates: 13g, Fiber: 4g, Total Fat: 18g, Saturated Fat: 3g, Cholesterol: 75mg, Sodium: 669mg

Mussels with Garlic and Wine

Serves 4   Prep time: 10 minutes   Cook time: 20 minutes

QUICK & EASY | GLUTEN-FREE   Mussels steamed in a flavored broth are available in the coastal villages all around the Mediterranean, with the ingredients in the broth changing from town to town or restaurant to restaurant. This recipe is a classic, made with wine and garlic. It can also be used with clams. I love eating this dish drizzled with Aioli (page 206) with slices of baguette to sop up the garlicky juices.

3 tablespoons extra-virgin olive oil

2 garlic cloves, minced

4 pounds mussels, scrubbed, beards removed

2 cups white wine

1 teaspoon salt

1 tablespoon chopped fresh flatleaf parsley

❋ The mussels need to be absolutely fresh for this dish, so be prepared to serve mussels the same day you buy them. When choosing mussels, make sure they are all tightly closed. They may open a tad as you travel home with them. Plunge them into a bowl of cool water when you get home, which should make them close again. Any mussels that don't close should be discarded.

1. Place a large Dutch oven or a heavy pot with a lid over high heat.

2. Add the oil and garlic and sauté for 1 minute.

3. Add the cleaned mussels, wine, and salt. Cover and bring to a boil. Reduce to a simmer and steam the mussels 3 to 4 minutes, or until the mussels have all opened.

4. Discard any unopened mussels.

5. Serve the mussels with their juices in a large bowl, garnished with chopped parsley.

PER SERVING Calories: 581, Protein: 54g, Total Carbohydrates: 21g, Fiber: 0g, Total Fat: 21g, Saturated Fat: 3g, Cholesterol: 127mg, Sodium: 1885mg

Scallops with Balsamic Dressing

Serves 4   Prep time: 10 minutes   Cook time: 20 minutes

QUICK & EASY | GLUTEN-FREE   My husband loves scallops, and this one-pan dish cooks in no time. First the scallops are seared and removed; next the rice is cooked in the same pan, followed by the spinach; then the scallops are returned to be heated through, and a balsamic sauce is poured over all. Balsamic vinegar is often used as a digestive aid in Italy.

2 tablespoons butter

4 tablespoons extra-virgin olive oil, divided

12 large sea scallops, trimmed of the muscles

1 cup rice

2 cups water

1 teaspoon salt

¼ teaspoon freshly ground black pepper

1 (5-ounce) bag spinach

1 tablespoon lemon zest

2 tablespoons lemon juice

1 tablespoon balsamic vinegar

❄ This dish is best when made and served immediately. It can be served at room temperature as a salad instead of a hot dish. If you're serving it that way, add the oil and balsamic vinegar right before serving.

1. Place a large skillet over high heat. Add the butter and 2 tablespoons olive oil.

2. When the butter has melted and the pan is very hot, add the scallops, quickly searing all sides, about 1 minute per side. Remove from the pan and set aside.

3. Add the rice to the same pan and stir to coat the rice with the juices in the pan.

4. Add the water, salt, and pepper, and bring to a boil. Reduce to a simmer, cover, and cook 15 to 30 minutes, or until all the water is absorbed and the rice is tender.

5. Turn off the heat and carefully stir the spinach into the hot rice. The rice will cook and wilt the spinach.

6. Return the scallops to the pan, add the lemon zest and juice, and cover. Let it sit on the stove with the heat off for 5 minutes.

7. Arrange the rice mixture on a serving platter.

8. Whisk the remaining 2 tablespoons olive oil and balsamic vinegar together and pour over the scallops and rice. Serve.

PER SERVING Calories: 431, Protein: 20g, Total Carbohydrates: 41g, Fiber: 2g, Total Fat: 21g, Saturated Fat: 6g, Cholesterol: 45mg, Sodium: 799mg

Shrimp Scampi

Serves 4   Prep time: 15 minutes   Cook time: 10 minutes

QUICK & EASY | GLUTEN-FREE   When I think of old-school Italian restaurants, I think of scampi. Mom would read every item on the menu and always settle for the scampi. I'm not sure why it fell from favor, because it is delicious. I like the combination of butter and olive oil in this recipe; the butter adds a nuttiness and the olive oil a fruity finish.

2 tablespoons extra-virgin olive oil

2 tablespoons butter

1½ pounds jumbo shrimp, peeled and deveined

1 large garlic clove, minced

¼ cup dry vermouth

1 teaspoon salt

1 tablespoon lemon zest

2 tablespoons lemon juice

1 tablespoon fresh chopped flatleaf parsley

❋ Scampi can be served as a first course or an appetizer, or it can be spooned over linguini for a pasta supper. This dish can also be made with scallops instead of shrimp.

1. Heat the olive oil in a large skillet over high heat. Add the butter.

2. When the butter has melted, add the shrimp and garlic and sauté for 1 minute.

3. Add the vermouth and salt and simmer for 5 minutes, or until the shrimp is cooked through and most of the liquid has evaporated.

4. Remove from the heat and add the lemon zest, juice, and parsley, and serve. This dish is best when made and served immediately.

PER SERVING Calories: 252, Protein: 31g, Total Carbohydrates: 1g, Fiber: 0g, Total Fat: 13g, Saturated Fat: 5g, Cholesterol: 365mg, Sodium: 2599mg

Shrimp and Greek Salad Pita

Serves 4   Prep time: 10 minutes   Cook time: 10 minutes

QUICK & EASY   I love this combination–warm pita bread spread with hummus and topped with cucumbers, tomatoes, prawns, and feta. It reminds me of the flavors of the falafel platter served at a local Israeli restaurant. It's dinner and a salad all in one. Round out the meal with a chilled glass of sparkling rosé.

2 tablespoons extra-virgin olive oil, plus more for drizzling

1 pound jumbo shrimp, peeled and deveined

1 teaspoon salt

¼ teaspoon freshly ground black pepper

4 pita breads

1 cup hummus (or Mashed Garbanzo Beans and Tahini, page 59)

16 thin slices cucumber

12 thin slices tomato

2 ounces feta cheese, crumbled

¼ cup chopped pitted Kalamata olives

¼ cup chopped fresh mint

❋ This dish can't be made ahead, but all the components can be prepped and ready for last-minute assembly. The shrimp can be served either hot or cold. To make your own pita bread, check out the recipe for Pork Souvlaki with Tzatziki on Pita Bread on page 102.

1. Preheat the oven to 350°F.

2. Heat the olive oil in a large skillet over high heat. Add the shrimp and sauté for 5 minutes, or until the shrimp are cooked through. Sprinkle with the salt and pepper and set aside.

3. Wrap the pita bread in foil and place in the oven to warm, about 5 to 7 minutes.

4. Remove the warm pitas from the oven and spread with hummus.

5. Top with cucumber slices, tomato slices, shrimp, feta, olives, and mint.

6. Drizzle each pita with olive oil and serve.

PER SERVING Calories: 471, Protein: 33g, Total Carbohydrates: 47g, Fiber: 6g, Total Fat: 18g, Saturated Fat: 4g, Cholesterol: 245mg, Sodium: 2692mg

Baked Shrimp with Ouzo and Tomatoes

Serves 4   Prep time: 10 minutes   Cook time: 10 minutes

QUICK & EASY | GLUTEN-FREE   Baked shrimp with ouzo and tomatoes is served in many restaurants throughout Greece, typically served sizzling in low-sided earthenware crocks. The licorice-like flavor of ouzo really complements the sweetness of the prawns. I like to serve this dish on top of a bed of fresh spinach, for a wilted salad.

¼ cup extra-virgin olive oil, plus more for drizzling

1 (14-ounce) can crushed tomatoes

1 clove garlic, minced

¼ cup ouzo

1 pound jumbo shrimp, peeled and deveined

1 teaspoon salt

¼ teaspoon freshly ground black pepper

1 teaspoon dried oregano

2 ounces feta cheese, crumbled

❋ Ouzo is an anise-flavored aperitif that is Greece's most popular drink. Anisette is a good substitute, or you can use white wine.

1. Preheat the oven to 400°F.

2. Pour the oil into a 9-inch pie plate and swirl to coat.

3. In a small bowl, combine the crushed tomatoes, garlic, and ouzo. Pour the mixture into the pie plate.

4. Arrange the shrimp on top. Sprinkle with the salt, pepper, and oregano. Add the feta.

5. Bake 7 to 10 minutes, or until the shrimp are cooked through.

6. Drizzle with olive oil before serving.

7. The cooked shrimp can be stored in the refrigerator for 3 days.

PER SERVING Calories: 319, Protein: 25g, Total Carbohydrates: 14g, Fiber: 3g, Total Fat: 16g, Saturated Fat: 4g, Cholesterol: 245mg, Sodium: 2247m

ten

Poultry & Meat

Chicken Legs with Herbs and Feta

Serves 4   Prep time: 15 minutes   Cook time: 40 minutes, plus 30 minutes or up to 2 days to marinate

GLUTEN-FREE   I like cooking with chicken legs and thighs with the bone in, because the chicken is always moist. For best results, let the chicken marinate overnight; it adds flavor and gives you a leg up for dinner the next day. Although I use preserved lemons in this dish, fresh lemons will work as well. I serve this simple family supper with buttered noodles and steamed broccoli.

8 chicken drumsticks
¼ cup extra-virgin olive oil
¼ cup white wine
¼ cup lemon juice
2 garlic cloves, minced
1 teaspoon dried oregano
1 teaspoon salt
¼ teaspoon freshly ground
    black pepper
1 ounce feta cheese, cut into
    small strips
6 thin wedges Preserved Lemons
    (page 148) or fresh lemon wedges
1 tablespoon grated lemon zest
1 tablespoon chopped fresh oregano

❋ Ideally, remove the marinating chicken from the refrigerator and let it sit at room temperature for 30 minutes before cooking. If the chicken isn't cold, it will cook more evenly.

1. Place the chicken, olive oil, wine, lemon juice, garlic, dried oregano, salt, and pepper into a 9-by-13-inch roasting pan, cover, and marinate for 30 minutes or overnight in the refrigerator. The chicken can marinate 2 days before cooking.

2. Preheat the oven to 375°F.

3. Uncover and cook the chicken for 35 to 45 minutes, or until it is golden brown.

4. Place the strips of feta on top of the chicken and tuck the preserved or fresh lemon wedges around it. Return to the oven for 5 to 7 minutes more to soften the feta and release the juices from the lemon.

5. Top with lemon zest and fresh oregano, and serve.

6. The cooked chicken will last 1 week in the refrigerator.

PER SERVING Calories: 306, Protein: 27g, Total Carbohydrates: 3g, Fiber: 1g, Total Fat: 20g, Saturated Fat: 4g, Cholesterol: 87mg, Sodium: 739mg

Turkish Chicken Kebabs

Serves 4 to 6   Prep time: 40 minutes   Cook time: 20 minutes, plus 30 minutes or overnight to marinate

GLUTEN-FREE | BIG 8 ALLERGEN-FRIENDLY   This is a great make-ahead recipe, since it's best if the meat marinates overnight. I've chosen chicken, but this recipe can be made with beef or lamb. The trick is to cut the vegetables and chicken pieces about the same size, so they are easy to turn. These skewers are perfect with Tzatziki (page 210) and warm Pitas (page 102) or naan bread.

2 white onions, chopped

2 garlic cloves, crushed

¾ cup extra-virgin olive oil, divided

2 tablespoons lemon juice

1 teaspoon dried oregano

2 teaspoons salt, divided

½ teaspoon curry powder

½ teaspoon ground turmeric

1½ pounds boneless chicken breast or
    thigh meat, cut into 1-inch pieces

12 skewers

2 red onions, cut into 1-inch pieces

3 to 4 zucchini, cut into 1-inch rounds

¼ teaspoon freshly ground
    black pepper

½ lemon

1 tablespoon chopped fresh mint

❋ You can make a fast and simple warm salad by removing the meat and vegetables from the skewers and arranging them over a bed of greens. Dress with Tzatziki (page 210).

1. Place the onions, garlic, ½ cup olive oil, lemon juice, oregano, 1 teaspoon salt, curry powder, and turmeric in a blender or food processor and process until puréed.

2. Place the chicken in a medium bowl, pour the marinade over, cover, and marinate in the refrigerator for at least 30 minutes, or overnight.

3. Thread the skewers by beginning with a piece of red onion, a piece of chicken, a piece of zucchini, a piece of chicken, and another piece of red onion. Place the skewers on a baking sheet.

4. When all the skewers have been made, brush with the remaining ¼ cup olive oil and sprinkle with 1 teaspoon salt and the pepper.

5. Heat a grill or broiler until hot. Cook the skewers over a hot grill or in a broiler until the meat is cooked, about 6 to 8 minutes per side. ❖

6. Season the cooked kebabs with freshly squeezed lemon juice and garnish with chopped mint.

7. Let the kebabs sit for about 5 minutes before serving.

8. After the meat has marinated, the skewers can be made and kept in the refrigerator for several hours before grilling. Once cooked, the chicken can be stored in the refrigerator for about 1 week.

PER SERVING Calories: 540, Protein: 53g, Total Carbohydrates: 17g, Fiber: 4g, Total Fat: 30g, Saturated Fat: 6g, Cholesterol: 151mg, Sodium: 1331mg

Chicken Fra Diavolo

Serves 4 to 6   Prep time: 15 minutes   Cook time: 50 minutes

GLUTEN-FREE | BIG 8 ALLERGEN-FRIENDLY   *Fra Diavolo* means "brother devil," and refers to the red pepper flakes in the sauce. You can make the sauce as spicy or mild as you'd like. The sauce is typically made with tomatoes, but can be made with red pepper flakes only. Smoked paprika is available in specialty grocery stores; if you can't find it, regular paprika will do. This dish tastes better when made ahead, which makes it great for entertaining. I like to eat it with a nice hunk of bread to sop up the sauce, but it's often served over pasta.

8 chicken thighs, skin on and bone in

1 teaspoon salt

¼ teaspoon freshly ground black pepper

¼ cup extra-virgin olive oil

1 large onion, sliced

3 garlic cloves, minced

1 teaspoon red pepper flakes (or to taste)

1 teaspoon smoked paprika

1 cup red wine

1 (14.5-ounce) can fire-roasted tomatoes

1 teaspoon dried oregano

2 tablespoons chopped fresh flatleaf parsley

❋ You can substitute pork chops for the chicken in this recipe. Thick bone-in pork chops are best for this dish.

1. Sprinkle the chicken with the salt and pepper.

2. Place a Dutch oven or a heavy pot with a lid over high heat. Add the olive oil and brown the chicken on all sides, about 3 to 4 minutes a side. Remove the chicken and set aside.

3. Place the onion, garlic, red pepper flakes, and paprika in the same pot and cook about 3 minutes to soften the onion. Add the wine, tomatoes, and oregano and bring to a boil.

4. Reduce to a simmer and return the chicken to the pot. Cover and simmer about 40 minutes or until the chicken is firm.

5. Arrange on a serving platter, garnish with parsley, and serve.

6. The sauce can be made ahead, without the chicken, and stored in the freezer. The entire dish can be stored for 1 week in the refrigerator or for several months in the freezer. Since the recipe makes a fairly large quantity, it's best to freeze it in single or double portions.

PER SERVING Calories: 670, Protein: 36g, Total Carbohydrates: 11g, Fiber: 3g, Total Fat: 51g, Saturated Fat: 16g, Cholesterol: 196mg, Sodium: 1010mg

Chicken Cacciatori

Serves 4 to 6   Prep time: 10 minutes   Cook time: 4 hours

GLUTEN-FREE | BIG 8 ALLERGEN-FREE   This dish brings back memories of a house filled with the aroma of Sunday suppers simmering in a pot. Using bone-in chicken makes the sauce more flavorful, and letting it have a long simmer in a slow cooker makes it trouble-free. I love serving Chicken Cacciatori over polenta with a dusting of Parmesan cheese.

8 chicken thighs, skin on and bone in

1 teaspoon salt

¼ teaspoon freshly ground
   black pepper

2 tablespoons extra-virgin olive oil

1 onion, chopped

1 red bell pepper, seeded
   and chopped

3 garlic cloves, sliced

½ cup red wine

1 (28-ounce) can crushed tomatoes

1 cup chicken broth or water

1 tablespoon capers

2 teaspoons dried oregano

※ You can substitute beef short ribs for the chicken in this recipe. Once cooked, remove the bones and you have a hearty sauce for pasta.

1. Sprinkle the chicken with the salt and pepper, and place in the bottom of a slow cooker.

2. Combine the olive oil, onion, bell pepper, garlic, red wine, tomatoes, chicken broth or water, capers, and oregano and pour over the chicken.

3. Cover and cook on high for 4 hours.

4. This is a hearty recipe that can last 1 week in the refrigerator or for several months in the freezer. Since it makes a big pot, it's good to freeze it in single servings for a fast lunch or supper.

PER SERVING Calories: 572, Protein: 41g, Total Carbohydrates: 23g, Fiber: 8g, Total Fat: 32g, Saturated Fat: 9g, Cholesterol: 130mg, Sodium: 1361mg

Chicken Thighs in Mushroom Red Wine Sauce

Serves 4 to 6 Prep time: 15 minutes Cook time: 4 hours

GLUTEN-FREE | BIG 8 ALLERGEN-FRIENDLY Bone-in chicken thighs are best for this recipe, since the bone keeps the chicken moist and flavorful and thighs are almost impossible to overcook. The long cook in a slow cooker turns the mushrooms and red wine into a delicious, rich sauce. I love serving this dish over mashed potatoes with a robust red wine. I like to brown the chicken before placing it in the slow cooker, since browning it adds flavor and color, but if you don't have the time, you can skip that step.

2 tablespoons extra-virgin olive oil

8 chicken thighs, skin on and bone in

1 teaspoon salt

¼ teaspoon freshly ground black pepper

3 shallots, thinly sliced

1 pound mushrooms, thinly sliced

1 cup red wine

1 cup chicken broth

1 sprig fresh thyme

❋ If you don't have a slow cooker, brown the chicken in a Dutch oven or a heavy pot with a lid. Remove the chicken and set it aside. Add the shallots and mushrooms to the same pot and sauté for 5 minutes. Add the wine, broth, salt, pepper, and thyme, and return the chicken to the pot. Bring to a boil, cover, and reduce to a simmer. Simmer for 1 hour.

1. Place a large skillet over high heat. Add the olive oil and cook the chicken until browned on all sides, about 3 to 4 minutes per side.

2. Transfer the chicken and all the pan juices to a slow cooker. Sprinkle with the salt and pepper.

3. Add the shallots, mushrooms, red wine, chicken broth, and thyme to the slow cooker.

4. Cover and cook on high for 4 hours.

5. Remove the thyme sprig and serve.

6. This recipe can be stored in the refrigerator 1 week, or frozen for several months. Since this makes a big quantity, it's best to freeze it in single or double potions for easy meals.

PER SERVING Calories: 403, Protein: 56g, Total Carbohydrates: 7g, Fiber: 1g, Total Fat: 13g, Saturated Fat: 2g, Cholesterol: 130mg, Sodium: 759mg

Chicken Almond Phyllo Pie

Serves 6 to 8   Prep time: 30 minutes   Cook time: 35 minutes

I first had this dish in Morocco, where it's called B'stilla and is made with pigeon. It blew me away to see ground poultry and spices cooked in phyllo, dusted with powdered sugar and ground almonds, and decorated with cinnamon like a little cake. It's both sweet and savory, and absolutely outstanding! In Morocco, making this dish is a real production. I've simplified it by using boneless chicken so it will cook faster. Find premade frozen phyllo (*filo* in Greek) in the frozen food aisle; defrost it in the fridge to prevent condensation.

2 tablespoons butter

2 tablespoons extra-virgin olive oil

1 large onion, chopped

2 garlic cloves, chopped

1¾ teaspoons ground cinnamon, divided

1 teaspoon cayenne pepper

1 teaspoon powdered ginger

½ teaspoon ground turmeric

¼ cup chicken broth or water

1 pound boneless chicken thigh meat, chopped into ¼-inch pieces

1 teaspoon salt

¼ teaspoon freshly ground black pepper

¼ cup finely chopped Preserved Lemons (page 148) or 2 tablespoons lemon juice

¼ cup chopped fresh flatleaf parsley

4 eggs, beaten

1 cup ground unsalted almonds

2 tablespoons sugar

6 ounces butter, melted

12 sheets phyllo (filo)

⅓ cup powdered sugar

1. Place a Dutch oven or a heavy pot with a lid over high heat and add the butter and olive oil.

2. Add the onion and garlic and sauté several minutes. Add 1 teaspoon cinnamon, the cayenne, ginger, and turmeric and sauté 5 minutes.

3. To the pot, add the broth, chicken, salt, and pepper, and simmer 10 minutes or until the chicken is cooked through and the liquid has evaporated. Remove the chicken from the pot and place in a large bowl. Let cool at least 15 minutes.

4. Add the preserved lemons or lemon juice, parsley, and eggs. Set aside.

5. In a small bowl, combine the ground almonds, sugar, and ½ teaspoon cinnamon and set aside.

6. Preheat the oven to 375°F.

7. Brush a 9-by-13-inch baking pan with a little melted butter.

8. Place 1 sheet of phyllo in the buttered pan and brush with more butter. Top with another layer of phyllo and brush with butter, then add a third layer and brush with butter.

9. Sprinkle one-half of the almond mixture over the phyllo. Top with three more sheets of phyllo, brushing each sheet with butter. Spoon one-half of the chicken over the phyllo. Top with three sheets of phyllo, brushing in between each sheet with butter. Add the remaining almond mixture. Finish the dish with the remaining chicken followed by the last three sheets of phyllo, brushing with butter in between each sheet.

10. Brush the top layer with butter. Using a sharp knife, score the top layers of phyllo into 12 pieces. This will prevent the phyllo from cracking as it rises in the oven.

11. Bake for 25 to 35 minutes or until golden brown. Remove from the oven and let cool for 10 minutes. Sprinkle with powdered sugar and the remaining ¼ teaspoon cinnamon. Serve warm.

❋ The number of ingredients is daunting, but it's really not complicated. There are three elements: the chicken filling, the almond filling, and the phyllo. The fillings can be made ahead for last-minute assembly, or the whole dish can be made ahead and frozen uncooked for several months. It can go from freezer to oven; this will extend the baking time, since the filling will be frozen. Garnish with the powdered sugar and cinnamon after baking.

PER SERVING Calories: 759, Protein: 34g, Total Carbohydrates: 48g, Fiber: 4g, Total Fat: 49g, Saturated Fat: 21g, Cholesterol: 248mg, Sodium: 960mg

Oven-Poached Chicken with Tarragon

Serves 4   Prep time: 10 minutes   Cook time: 25 to 35 minutes

GLUTEN-FREE | BIG 8 ALLERGEN-FRIENDLY   Oven poaching boneless, skinless breasts results in moist and tender meat, infused with flavor–in this case, tarragon. If you're serving this dish warm, pair the chicken with Salsa Verde (page 150) or Romanesco Sauce (page 147). If you're serving it cold, add a dollop of Aioli (page 206) on the side. Either way, boiled new potatoes and green beans complement the flavors perfectly.

6 boneless, skinless chicken breasts

½ cup white wine

1 cup chicken broth or water

1 shallot, sliced

3 sprigs fresh tarragon, plus
    1 teaspoon chopped for garnish

1 teaspoon salt

¼ teaspoon freshly ground
    black pepper

✳ Save the poaching liquid, since it's loaded with flavor and can be used to make sauces and soups. The liquid can be kept in a jar and frozen until you're ready to use it.

1. Preheat the oven to 375°F.

2. Place the chicken breasts in a single layer in a 9-by-13-inch pan.

3. Add the wine, broth or water, shallot, tarragon sprigs, salt, and pepper. Gently stir to combine ingredients.

4. Cover with foil and place in the oven for 25 to 35 minutes, or until the chicken is firm to the touch.

5. Carefully remove the foil, since it will release hot steam. Let the chicken rest 10 minutes in the poaching liquid before serving.

6. Remove the chicken from the pan with a slotted spoon and garnish with the chopped tarragon.

7. Poached chicken can be stored in the refrigerator for 1 week.

PER SERVING Calories: 358, Protein: 51g, Total Carbohydrates: 1g, Fiber: 0g, Total Fat: 13g, Saturated Fat: 4g, Cholesterol: 151mg, Sodium: 920mg

Moroccan Chicken with Oranges and Olives

Serves 4   Prep time: 10 minutes   Cook time: 20 minutes

QUICK & EASY | GLUTEN-FREE | BIG 8 ALLERGEN-FREE   I really like using salt-cured olives in this recipe because they have a more traditional Middle Eastern flavor. They are slightly shriveled and have a very intense salty, briny taste, though, that some people don't like. Salt-cured olives are most easily found at the olive bar of specialty markets or Middle Eastern delis. They are sometimes called Moroccan olives. Feel free to substitute another type of olive if you prefer. Serve over a fluffy bed of Couscous with Roasted Vegetables (page 128).

½ cup rice flour
1 teaspoon ground cumin
1 teaspoon ground ginger
1 teaspoon ground cinnamon
½ teaspoon salt
¼ teaspoon freshly ground
   black pepper
4 boneless, skinless chicken breasts
3 tablespoons extra-virgin olive oil
1 garlic clove, thinly sliced
½ cup wine
½ cup chicken broth or water
Several saffron threads
½ cup salt-cured olives
1 orange, sliced
¼ cup chopped fresh cilantro

❋ If you don't like the sweet-salty combination of oranges and olives, you can omit the olives and add ½ cup chopped dried apricots instead.

1. Combine the rice flour, cumin, ginger, cinnamon, salt, and pepper in a small shallow bowl.

2. Dredge each piece of chicken in the spice mixture.

3. Place a large skillet over high heat and add the olive oil. Add the chicken and brown on all sides, about 3 to 4 minutes per side.

4. Add the garlic, wine, broth or water, and saffron to the pan and bring to a boil. Reduce to a simmer and cook for 15 minutes.

5. Add the olives and orange slices, cover, and turn off the heat. Let it sit for 5 minutes to combine the flavors.

6. Remove the lid, add the cilantro, and serve.

7. This dish can be stored for 5 days in the refrigerator.

PER SERVING Calories: 443, Protein: 35g, Total Carbohydrates: 24g, Fiber: 2g, Total Fat: 21g, Saturated Fat: 4g, Cholesterol: 101mg, Sodium: 487mg

Spanish Almond Chicken

Serves 4   Prep time: 15 minutes   Cook time: 30 minutes

GLUTEN-FREE   Pan-fried chicken is served here with a sauce made from almonds and spices. This has many of the flavors in the Chicken Almond Phyllo Pie (page 168) but is a fraction of the work. I like serving this with Roasted Carrots with Anise (page 65) and a simple salad of spinach dressed with lemon juice and sea salt to balance the richness of the almond sauce.

1 tablespoon extra-virgin olive oil

1 tablespoon butter

4 boneless, skinless chicken breasts

½ medium onion, sliced

1 garlic clove, sliced

¼ cup blanched (skinless) unsalted almonds

½ teaspoon ground cinnamon

½ teaspoon ground nutmeg

¼ teaspoon ground turmeric

½ cup chicken broth

¼ cup dry sherry

1 teaspoon salt

¼ teaspoon freshly ground black pepper

1 tablespoon chopped fresh flatleaf parsley

❋ The sauce can be made several days ahead, and is best reheated very gently over a very low flame or in the top of a double boiler.

1. Place a large skillet over high heat. Add the olive oil and butter and cook the chicken breasts on all sides until firm, about 5 to 7 minutes per side. Remove the chicken and set aside.

2. Add the onion, garlic, almonds, cinnamon, nutmeg, and turmeric to the same pan and sauté until the almonds are lightly browned, about 1 to 2 minutes.

3. Place the almond mixture, chicken broth, sherry, salt, and pepper in a blender or food processor and process until the mixture is smooth. If the sauce is too thick, add additional chicken broth to get the consistency of heavy cream.

4. Return the chicken to the pan and add the almond sauce. Reduce the heat to low and let the sauce warm through. Be careful not to simmer the sauce, because it will separate.

5. Arrange the chicken and sauce on a serving platter, top with parsley, and serve.

6. This recipe can be stored in the refrigerator for 4 days.

PER SERVING Calories: 334, Protein: 35g, Total Carbohydrates: 4g, Fiber: 1g, Total Fat: 18g, Saturated Fat: 5g, Cholesterol: 109mg, Sodium: 710mg

Chicken Breast Stuffed with Sun-Dried Tomatoes and Ricotta

Serves 4   Prep time: 30 minutes   Cook time: 45 minutes

GLUTEN-FREE   This dish looks much harder than it is, and will wow your friends with your culinary prowess! Sun-dried tomatoes and ricotta are combined, tucked under the skin of the chicken breast, and baked. This was a staple when I did catering. What I like about it is as comfortable on the buffet table as it is on a dinner plate.

4 ounces ricotta cheese

2 tablespoons chopped sun-dried tomatoes

1 garlic clove, chopped

½ teaspoon chopped fresh thyme

1½ teaspoons salt, divided

4 boneless, skin-on chicken breasts

2 tablespoons extra-virgin olive oil

¼ teaspoon freshly ground black pepper

1 cup white wine

½ lemon

❋ You can stuff the breasts several hours ahead and roast them later. For best results, let them sit 30 minutes at room temperature before cooking them. It's important to let the chicken breasts rest after they've been baked as well, because if you cut them while they are very hot, the ricotta will ooze out.

1. Preheat the oven to 375°F.

2. In a small bowl, combine the ricotta, sun-dried tomatoes, garlic, thyme, and ½ teaspoon salt.

3. Place the chicken skin side up on a work surface.

4. Slide your fingers under the skin and gently pull the skin partially away from the chicken breast, being careful not to tear it.

5. Place about 2 tablespoons of filling under the skin of each breast.

6. Place the stuffed breasts, skin side up, in a 9-inch-square baking dish, tucking the ends of the breasts under so that the breasts are plump and round.

7. Brush the breasts with olive oil and sprinkle with the remaining 1 teaspoon salt and the pepper.

8. Pour the wine into the pan, and bake 35 to 45 minutes or until the skin is golden brown.

9. Remove from the oven and squeeze the lemon juice over the stuffed breasts.

10. Let rest 10 minutes before serving.

11. The breasts can be stored in the refrigerator for 5 days.

PER SERVING Calories: 359, Protein: 37g, Total Carbohydrates: 4g, Fiber: 1g, Total Fat: 17g, Saturated Fat: 4g, Cholesterol: 139mg, Sodium: 1415mg

Chicken Roasted with 40 Cloves of Garlic

Serves 4   Prep time: 15 minutes   Cook time: 75 minutes

GLUTEN-FREE | BIG 8 ALLERGEN-FRIENDLY   This is a classic dish that was commonly served by home cooks throughout the French countryside. Don't be put off by the amount of garlic. The whole cloves become mellow and sweet as they roast–plus they fill your home with a lovely garlic aroma. Since the oven will be on for the chicken, I like to throw some zucchini in to roast as well. Serve the chicken with thick slices of French bread to spread with the soft roasted garlic.

1 whole chicken

1 teaspoon salt

¼ teaspoon freshly ground black pepper

2 tablespoons butter

2 tablespoons extra-virgin olive oil

40 garlic cloves (about 3 to 4 heads), peeled

1 cup white wine

1 sprig fresh thyme

❈ Some markets sell peeled garlic. If yours doesn't, there are several ways to easily remove the skin. One is to blanch the garlic in boiling water for a minute, drain it, and slip off the skins. Another technique is to use a garlic roller—a rubber tube you place the garlic inside and roll, pressing down, to release the skins from the cloves. Garlic rollers are available in some grocery stores, online, and in cookware stores.

1. Preheat the oven to 375°F.

2. Pat the chicken dry with a paper towel and sprinkle with the salt and pepper.

3. Place a large Dutch oven or a heavy pot with a lid over high heat. Add the butter and olive oil. Brown the chicken on all sides, about 5 to 7 minutes per side, using tongs to carefully turn it without breaking the skin.

4. Remove the chicken and set aside.

5. Add the garlic to the same pot and sauté for 5 minutes to soften. Return the chicken to the pot and add the wine and thyme.

6. Cover the pot and place it in the oven for 1 hour.

7. Carefully remove the chicken from the pot and let it rest for 15 minutes.

8. Carve the chicken and arrange it on a platter. Remove the thyme sprig. Spoon the garlic and pan drippings over the chicken and serve.

PER SERVING Calories: 722, Protein: 48g, Total Carbohydrates: 4g, Fiber: 0g, Total Fat: 51g, Saturated Fat: 16g, Cholesterol: 250mg, Sodium: 809mg

Pork Loin Gremolata

Serves 4 to 6   Prep time: 15 minutes   Cook time: 40 minutes

GLUTEN-FREE | BIG 8 ALLERGEN-FRIENDLY   This is a simple way to dress up any roast. I'm using pork in this recipe, but you can also use lamb, beef, or chicken. I like to serve this with Sweet and Sour Pumpkin with Pine Nuts and Raisins (page 70) and roasted potatoes. Leftovers make a fast and easy sandwich of sliced pork, gremolata, greens, and tomatoes on a ciabatta roll.

1 cup water

One 3- to 4-pound boneless pork loin roast

2 tablespoons extra-virgin olive oil, plus more to oil the roasting pan

1½ teaspoons salt

½ teaspoon freshly ground black pepper

¼ teaspoon ground nutmeg

1 recipe Gremolata (page 119)

❋ The pork loin can be seasoned several hours ahead and kept in the refrigerator until you're ready to cook. For best results, allow the pork loin to sit 30 minutes at room temperature before roasting.

1. Preheat the oven to 400°F.

2. Oil a roasting pan big enough to hold the pork roast. Add 1 cup water to the roasting pan.

3. Rub the roast with the olive oil and top with the salt, pepper, and nutmeg.

4. Roast 40 minutes, or until a meat thermometer reads 150°F.

5. Remove from the oven and let rest 10 to 15 minutes before serving.

6. To serve, cut the pork roast into ¼-inch slices and arrange on a platter. Spoon the gremolata over the top, or serve it on the side.

7. Roast pork will last in the refrigerator for about 1 week. Gremolata will last 1 week in the refrigerator or a few months in the freezer.

PER SERVING Calories: 576, Protein: 90g, Total Carbohydrates: 2g, Fiber: 1g, Total Fat: 22g, Saturated Fat: 6g, Cholesterol: 248mg, Sodium: 1365mg

Marsala Pork Chops with Figs

Serves 4   Prep time: 10 minutes   Cook time: 20 minutes

QUICK & EASY | GLUTEN-FREE | BIG 8 ALLERGEN-FRIENDLY   Marsala is a wine from the city of the same name in Sicily. It can be either sweet or dry, but in America we mostly use sweet Marsala, fortified so that it resembles port. Its spiciness lends itself well to this dish and pairs nicely with figs. The figs in this recipe are dried, but if you can get fresh figs, by all means use them! It you can find fresh figs, add them at the very end of the cooking time so they don't become mushy.

4 thick pork chops

2½ teaspoons salt, divided

½ teaspoon freshly ground
   black pepper

¼ teaspoon ground cinnamon

2 tablespoons extra-virgin olive oil,
   plus more to oil the pan

2 shallots, thinly sliced

¾ cup chicken or beef broth

⅓ cup Marsala wine

6 dried figs, stems cut off,
   cut in half

1 tablespoon chopped fresh
   flatleaf parsley

❋ This recipe can be made with chicken breasts, boneless chicken thighs, or lamb chops instead.

1. Sprinkle the pork chops with 1½ teaspoons salt, the pepper, and cinnamon.

2. Place the olive oil in a large skillet over high heat. Add the seasoned pork chops and cook until they are golden on both sides, about 4 minutes per side. Remove the chops and set aside.

3. Add the shallots to the same pan and sauté until they begin to brown, about 5 minutes.

4. Add the chicken or beef broth, wine, figs, and remaining 1 teaspoon salt and bring to a boil. Reduce to a simmer and return the pork chops to the pan.

5. Cover and cook the chops an additional 3 to 5 minutes, until they are cooked through.

6. Arrange the chops on a serving platter and spoon the Marsala sauce over the top. Garnish with the parsley.

7. The cooked chops can be stored up to 5 days in the refrigerator.

PER SERVING Calories: 523, Protein: 28g, Total Carbohydrates: 20g, Fiber: 3g, Total Fat: 36g, Saturated Fat: 12g, Cholesterol: 98mg, Sodium: 1681mg

Lamb Meatballs

Serves 4   Prep time: 15 minutes   Cook time: 15 minutes

QUICK & EASY | GLUTEN-FREE | BIG 8 ALLERGEN-FRIENDLY   My twist on spaghetti and meatballs is to serve lamb meatballs atop pesto pasta with crumbled feta cheese. Even people who don't care for lamb like lamb meatballs, but if you're not convinced, you can make yours with a mixture of 50-50 beef and lamb.

1 pound ground lamb

3 scallions, thinly sliced

2 garlic cloves, minced

3 tablespoons rice flour

1 egg

1 teaspoon dried oregano

1 teaspoon salt

½ teaspoon ground cumin

¼ teaspoon red pepper flakes (optional)

¼ teaspoon freshly ground black pepper

Oil to coat the baking sheet

❋ If you don't have rice flour, substitute all-purpose flour.

1. Preheat the oven to 400°F.

2. Place the ground lamb, scallions, garlic, rice flour, egg, oregano, salt, cumin, red pepper flakes (if using), and pepper in a medium bowl and mix well.

3. Oil a rimmed baking sheet. Using a 1-ounce ice cream scoop, scoop the meatballs and place them on the oiled baking sheet. Leave about 1 inch around each meatball on the sheet so they brown nicely.

4. Bake for 12 to 15 minutes or until the meatballs are firm.

5. Arrange on a platter and serve.

6. These meatballs can be stored in the refrigerator for 1 week or frozen for several months.

PER SERVING Calories: 262, Protein: 34g, Total Carbohydrates: 8g, Fiber: 1g, Total Fat: 10g, Saturated Fat: 3g, Cholesterol: 143mg, Sodium: 686mg

Mediterranean Lamb Stew

Serves 4 to 6   Prep time: 15 minutes   Cook time: 4 hours

GLUTEN-FREE | BIG 8 ALLERGEN-FRIENDLY   Rich, fragrant with spices, and simmered in wine, this stew will transport you to your private corner of the Mediterranean. When I make it, I like to imagine I'm strolling the winding streets of a Mediterranean village. Ladle this delicious stew over a fluffy mound of couscous or basmati rice.

3 pounds lamb stew meat

2 onions, chopped

2 garlic cloves, minced

3 tablespoons extra-virgin olive oil

1 (28-ounce) can crushed tomatoes

1 cup red wine

1 (5-ounce) can tomato paste

½ cup chopped dried apricots

1 bay leaf

1½ teaspoons dried oregano

1½ teaspoons ground cumin

1 teaspoon salt

½ teaspoon freshly ground
    black pepper

1 cinnamon stick

3 tablespoons honey

2 tablespoons orange zest

¼ cup chopped fresh cilantro

❋ This stew can be made with pork instead of lamb. Like almost all stews, it will be even better the next day.

1. Place the lamb, onions, garlic, olive oil, tomatoes, wine, tomato paste, apricots, bay leaf, oregano, cumin, salt, pepper, cinnamon stick, and honey in a slow cooker. Stir to combine the ingredients.

2. Cover and cook on high for 4 hours.

3. Stir in the orange zest and cilantro and serve.

4. Store in the refrigerator for 1 week, or for several months in the freezer.

PER SERVING Calories: 970, Protein: 103g, Total Carbohydrates: 58g, Fiber: 10g, Total Fat: 36g, Saturated Fat: 11g, Cholesterol: 306mg, Sodium: 1264mg

Pomegranate-Glazed Lamb Shanks

Serves 4 to 6   Prep time: 15 minutes   Cook time: 6 hours

GLUTEN-FREE | BIG 8 ALLERGEN-FRIENDLY   Lamb shanks were a frequent Sunday-night supper. I always thought of them as little legs of lamb. They have the same buttery flavor as leg of lamb, but cook much more quickly since they are smaller. The cooking is long and slow here in a slow cooker. The pomegranate glaze provides a tangy sweetness and a beautiful deep mahogany color.

4 lamb shanks, about 1 pound each

2 teaspoons salt

1 teaspoon paprika

½ teaspoon freshly ground
   black pepper

1 onion, chopped

2 carrots, peeled and chopped

2 garlic cloves, minced

2 tablespoons extra-virgin olive oil

1 cup pomegranate juice

¼ cup honey

1 tablespoon orange zest

¼ cup chopped fresh flatleaf parsley

❄ Pomegranate juice can be expensive; you can substitute cranberry or cherry juice instead.

1. Season the lamb shanks with the salt, paprika, and pepper and place in a slow cooker.

2. Add the onion, carrots, garlic, olive oil, pomegranate juice, and honey. Mix well.

3. Cover and cook on low for 6 hours.

4. Add the orange zest and parsley and serve.

5. Lamb shanks can be stored for 1 week in the refrigerator, or frozen for several months. For easier defrosting, it's best to remove the meat from the bone before freezing.

PER SERVING Calories: 883, Protein: 64g, Total Carbohydrates: 34g, Fiber: 2g, Total Fat: 52g, Saturated Fat: 22g, Cholesterol: 240mg, Sodium: 1431mg

Stuffed Peppers

Serves 6   Prep time: 15 minutes   Cook time: 45 minutes

GLUTEN-FREE | BIG 8 ALLERGEN-FRIENDLY   Peppers stuffed with meat and rice are a classic, and always make me think of my grandmother, who loved to make them. I've used a mixture of beef and lamb in this recipe, but beef and pork also work well. It's traditional to use green bell peppers in this dish, but feel free to substitute red, yellow, or orange if you prefer. The leftovers make handy work lunches since they travel easily.

3 tablespoons extra-virgin olive oil
1 large white onion, chopped
½ pound ground lamb
½ pound ground beef
1 tablespoon chopped sun-dried
    tomatoes (optional)
1 garlic clove, minced
1 teaspoon salt
1 teaspoon dried oregano
¼ teaspoon freshly ground
    black pepper
2 cups cooked rice
1 (7.5-ounce) can tomato sauce
2 tablespoons chopped fresh
    flatleaf parsley
6 large green bell peppers, tops
    removed and reserved,
    seeds discarded
1 cup chicken broth or water

❋ The peppers can be made several hours or 1 day ahead and baked right before serving. For best results, let them sit at room temperature for 30 minutes before cooking.

1. Preheat the oven to 350°F.

2. Place a large skillet over high heat. Add the olive oil and sauté the onion for 5 to 7 minutes, or until it begins to brown.

3. Add the lamb and beef and cook until there is no pink left in the meat. Drain any liquid from the pan.

4. Add the sun-dried tomatoes (if using), garlic, salt, oregano, black pepper, rice, tomato sauce, and parsley and cook 1 or 2 minutes to thicken the sauce.

5. Set the filling aside and let it sit for 10 to 15 minutes before stuffing the peppers.

6. Spoon the filling into the prepared peppers and place in a 9-by-13-inch roasting pan.

7. Top each pepper with its lid. Carefully pour the broth or water into the pan.

8. Bake 30 minutes or until the peppers are soft. Let them sit for 10 minutes before serving.

9. Cooked peppers can be stored in the refrigerator for 1 week or frozen for several months.

PER SERVING Calories: 374, Protein: 27g, Total Carbohydrates: 37g, Fiber: 5g, Total Fat: 13g, Saturated Fat: 3g, Cholesterol: 68mg, Sodium: 774mg

Tuscan Steak with Salsa Verde

Serves 4   Prep time: 10 minutes   Cook time: 20 minutes

QUICK & EASY | GLUTEN-FREE | BIG 8 ALLERGEN-FRIENDLY   Who doesn't like a big beautiful steak, pan-seared to capture the juices and served with a garlicky sauce? The secret of this dish is using a really hot pan (ideally a large cast iron skillet) and letting the meat rest for 10 to 15 minutes before serving. The steak is clearly the star of this meal, so I'd serve it simply with sliced ripe seasonal tomatoes, roasted fingerling potatoes, and a glass of bold red wine.

2 (18-ounce) bone-in rib eye steaks,
    about 1½ inches thick
2 tablespoons extra-virgin olive oil
1½ teaspoons salt
½ teaspoon freshly ground
    black pepper
1 recipe Salsa Verde (page 150)

❋ The steaks can be seasoned several hours before cooking and kept in the refrigerator. For best results, allow them to sit at room temperature before cooking.

1. Preheat the oven to 400°F.

2. Rub the steaks with the olive oil and sprinkle with salt and pepper.

3. Place a large heavy skillet over high heat and let the pan get hot. To test, flick a few drops of water onto the pan. The water should immediately pop and evaporate; that's how you know the pan is ready.

4. Place the steaks in the pan and brown for 3 to 4 minutes or until they are a deep golden brown on each side.

5. Place the steaks on a rimmed baking sheet and slide it into the oven. Cook 10 minutes for rare or 15 minutes for medium.

6. Remove from the oven and let rest 10 to 15 minutes. Slice thin and serve with Salsa Verde.

7. Once cooked, the steaks will keep for 5 days in the refrigerator.

PER SERVING Calories: 1205, Protein: 74g, Total Carbohydrates: 11g, Fiber: 3g, Total Fat: 98g, Saturated Fat: 18g, Cholesterol: 225mg, Sodium: 1984mg

Provençal Stew

Serves 4 to 6   Prep time: 10 minutes   Cook time: 4 hours

GLUTEN-FREE | BIG 8 ALLERGEN-FRIENDLY   Herbes de Provence and red wine are the key flavors of this stew. Typically, herbes de Provence is a dried herb mixture of savory, marjoram, rosemary, thyme, oregano, and lavender. It's available in the spice aisle of the grocery store, but if you can't find it, you can create your own spice blend using your favorite dried herbs. I'm using beef in this recipe, but lamb works nicely as well.

3 tablespoons extra-virgin olive oil

2 pounds beef stew meat

4 ounces pancetta or bacon, diced

1½ teaspoons salt

½ teaspoon freshly ground
  black pepper

2 leeks, root and top trimmed,
  thinly sliced

2 cloves garlic, thinly sliced

2 large zucchini, cut into 1-inch slices

1 pound mushrooms, halved

1 tablespoon tomato paste

1 teaspoon herbes de Provence

2 cups red wine

❈ This dish can be made several days ahead and reheated when you're ready to serve. Like most stews, it just keeps getting better.

1. Place the olive oil, beef, pancetta or bacon, salt, pepper, leeks, garlic, zucchini, mushrooms, tomato paste, herbes de Provence, and red wine in a slow cooker. Stir gently to combine.

2. Cover and cook on high for 4 hours.

3. This dish can be stored in the refrigerator for 1 week and frozen for several months. It's best to freeze soups and stews in single or double servings for easier thawing.

PER SERVING Calories: 846, Protein: 86g, Total Carbohydrates: 21g, Fiber: 4g, Total Fat: 37g, Saturated Fat: 11g, Cholesterol: 234mg, Sodium: 1718mg

Orange Beef Stew

Serves 6   Prep time: 15 minutes   Cook time: 4 hours, plus about 10 minutes browning the meat

GLUTEN-FREE | BIG 8 ALLERGEN-FRIENDLY   This is a slow cooker stew, but if you have the time, browning the meat first will add a rich, nutty flavor to the stew. Cumin and orange juice are the keynote flavors for this dish. Serve this over couscous or bulgur.

2 tablespoons extra-virgin olive oil

3 pounds beef stew meat

2 teaspoons salt, divided

¼ teaspoon freshly ground black pepper

1 large white onion, sliced

1 pound small whole mushrooms

2 large carrots, peeled and cut into 1-inch pieces

1 cup orange juice

Zest of 1 orange

2 garlic cloves, minced

1 (6-ounce) can tomato paste

¼ cup balsamic or red wine vinegar

3 tablespoons honey

2 teaspoons dried cumin

2 teaspoons dried oregano

½ teaspoon ground allspice

1 orange, sliced

¼ cup fresh chopped flatleaf parsley

❋ This recipe can be made ahead and reheated before serving. It's best not to add the oranges or parsley until you're ready to serve.

1. Place a large skillet over high heat and add the olive oil.

2. Season the meat with 1 teaspoon salt and the pepper and place it in the pan. Being careful not to crowd the meat (cook in batches if necessary), brown on all sides, about 2 to 3 minutes per side.

3. Place the browned meat in the slow cooker.

4. Add the onion, mushrooms, carrots, orange juice, orange zest, garlic, tomato paste, vinegar, honey, cumin, oregano, 1 teaspoon salt, and the allspice. Cover and cook on high for 4 hours.

5. Spoon the stew into serving bowl and garnish with orange slices and parsley.

6. This dish can be stored for 1 week in the refrigerator or frozen for several months. Freeze it in single or double portions for easy thawing and serving.

PER SERVING Calories: 595, Protein: 74g, Total Carbohydrates: 31g, Fiber: 4g, Total Fat: 20g, Saturated Fat: 6g, Cholesterol: 203mg, Sodium: 978mg

eleven

Snacks & Desserts

Toasted Pita Wedges with Sea Salt

Serves 6 to 8   Prep time: 10 minutes   Cook time: 10 to 15 minutes

QUICK & EASY | VEGAN   Since pita goes stale quickly, this is a good way to extend its shelf life and use up the whole package. Pita chips are great on their own, or dipped into sauces and spreads. They can also be used to make fattoush, a Levantine bread salad made with toasted pita, greens, herbs, and vegetables.

1 (12-ounce) package whole-wheat
   pita bread
¼ cup extra-virgin olive oil
1 teaspoon sea salt

❋ A coarse-grained sea salt, or kosher salt, is best for this dish. Regular table salt will not work well, since its fine texture means it won't stay on the chips. If you'd like to make your own pita bread from scratch, check out the recipe for Pork Souvlaki with Tzatziki on Pita Bread (page 102).

1. Preheat the oven to 375°F.

2. Cut each pita bread into 12 wedges.

3. Place the pita wedges in a large bowl and drizzle with the olive oil and sea salt.

4. Arrange the pita in a single layer on a baking sheet (you may need two) and place in the oven.

5. Toast the pita until crisp and lightly browned, about 10 to 15 minutes.

6. The pita wedges can be stored in an airtight container at room temperature for about 10 days.

PER SERVING Calories: 223, Protein: 6g, Total Carbohydrates: 31g, Fiber: 4g, Total Fat: 10g, Saturated Fat: 1g, Cholesterol: 0mg, Sodium: 614mg

Feta with Olive Oil and Herbs

Serves 4   Prep time: 10 minutes, plus 1 hour to marinate

QUICK & EASY | VEGETARIAN | GLUTEN-FREE   Whenever I visit a Greek home, I am served several snacks to nibble on while chatting. Often the snack is a thick slice of feta that has been marinated in olive oil and herbs. The longer you marinate the cheese, the stronger the flavor. Serve with sliced cucumbers or chunks of bread to soak up the marinade.

8 ounces feta cheese
¼ cup extra-virgin olive oil
1 tablespoon chopped fresh oregano
1 tablespoon red wine vinegar
2 teaspoons lemon zest
¼ teaspoon red pepper flakes

❋ You can add any spices, herbs, or aromatics (garlic and onion) that you'd like.

1. Place the feta in a shallow bowl.

2. Pour the olive oil over the feta and sprinkle with the oregano, vinegar, lemon zest, and pepper flakes.

3. Cover and marinate at room temperature for 1 hour before serving, or refrigerate for several days.

4. To serve, cut the feta into bite-size pieces.

5. The cheese will keep for 1 week in the refrigerator.

PER SERVING Calories: 263, Protein: 8g, Total Carbohydrates: 3g, Fiber: 1g, Total Fat: 25g, Saturated Fat: 10g, Cholesterol: 50mg, Sodium: 633mg

Sautéed Olives with Basil

Serves 6 to 8   Prep time: 10 minutes   Cook time: 5 minutes

QUICK & EASY | VEGAN | GLUTEN-FREE | BIG 8 ALLERGEN-FRIENDLY   I like to serve sautéed olives with cocktails, but I also enjoy them spooned hot over a salad or with lamb chops.

2 tablespoons extra-virgin olive oil

2 cups pitted olives (Kalamata and Sicilian or a pitted Greek blend)

⅛ teaspoon red pepper flakes (optional)

1 garlic clove, minced

1 scallion, thinly sliced

½ teaspoon dried rosemary

1 tablespoon slivered Preserved Lemons (page 148, optional)

❋ This dish is meant to be served warm. However, if you have leftovers, it's fine to serve them at room temperature.

1. Place a medium frying pan over high heat.

2. Add the olive oil, olives, red pepper flakes (if using), and garlic. Sauté 5 minutes or until the olives start to wilt.

3. Add the scallions, rosemary, and Preserved Lemon (if using). Serve warm.

4. Store leftovers in the refrigerator for up to 10 days.

PER SERVING Calories: 93, Protein: 1g, Total Carbohydrates: 3g, Fiber: 2g, Total Fat: 10g, Saturated Fat: 1g, Cholesterol: 0mg, Sodium: 391mg

Moroccan Zucchini Spread

Serves 4   Prep time: 10 minutes   Cook time: 20 minutes

QUICK & EASY | VEGAN | GLUTEN-FREE | BIG 8 ALLERGEN-FRIENDLY   Zucchini is roasted until fork tender and mashed with tahini, garlic, and herbs for this chunky spread. It's delicious eaten with crudités or with Toasted Pita Wedges with Sea Salt (page 186). Or serve it as a side dish to roasted lamb or chicken.

¼ cup plus 1 tablespoon extra-virgin olive oil, divided, plus more for drizzling

4 large zucchini, cut in half lengthwise

2 teaspoons salt, divided

¼ cup tahini

1 garlic clove, minced

¼ cup lemon juice

½ teaspoon dried oregano

¼ teaspoon cayenne pepper

2 scallions, thinly sliced

1 tablespoon chopped fresh mint

✿ You can make this recipe with any softer (when cooked) vegetable, such as eggplant, winter squash, or cauliflower.

1. Preheat the oven to 375°F.

2. Brush a baking sheet with olive oil.

3. Brush the zucchini with ¼ cup olive oil and sprinkle with 1 teaspoon salt. Place the zucchini skin side down on the oiled baking sheet.

4. Roast for 15 to 20 minutes or until the zucchini is so soft it can be mashed with a fork.

5. Place the zucchini in a medium bowl and mash with a fork or potato masher.

6. Mix in the tahini, garlic, 1 tablespoon olive oil, the lemon juice, 1 teaspoon salt, the oregano, and cayenne.

7. Add the scallions and mint and mix well.

8. Spoon the mixture into a serving bowl, drizzle with olive oil, and serve warm or at room temperature.

9. The spread will keep 5 days in the refrigerator or in the freezer for several months.

PER SERVING Calories: 300, Protein: 7g, Total Carbohydrates: 15g, Fiber: 5g, Total Fat: 26g, Saturated Fat: 4g, Cholesterol: 0mg, Sodium: 1217mg

Crostini with Mashed Fava Beans

Serves 4 to 6   Prep time: 10 minutes   Cook time: 10 minutes

QUICK & EASY | VEGAN   Using frozen fava beans makes this dish a snap! If you can't find frozen fava beans in your market, you can substitute the same amount of frozen and thawed peas or lima beans. The color is a beautiful bright green. If you can eat dairy, serve this dish with shaved Parmesan or crumbled feta on top.

1 whole-grain baguette, sliced into
    ¼-inch slices
¼ cup plus ⅓ cup extra-virgin
    olive oil, divided
2 teaspoons salt, divided
1 (10-ounce) package frozen
    fava beans, thawed
1 garlic clove, smashed
¼ cup lemon juice
¼ teaspoon freshly ground
    black pepper
1 tablespoon chopped fresh mint

❋ The crostini can be made several days ahead and stored in an airtight container at room temperature until ready to use. If they get soft, pop them into the oven to toast again.

1. Preheat the oven to 375°F.

2. Lay the bread slices on a baking sheet in a single layer (you may need two baking sheets).

3. Brush the bread with ¼ cup olive oil and sprinkle with 1 teaspoon salt.

4. Place the baking sheet in the oven and toast for about 10 to 12 minutes, or until lightly golden. Set aside.

5. Place the fava beans, garlic, ⅓ cup olive oil, lemon juice, 1 teaspoon salt, and the pepper in a food processor or blender and process until smooth. The spread will have a coarse texture.

6. Add the chopped mint. Spread the fava bean mixture on the cooled crostini and serve.

7. The fava bean spread can be stored in the refrigerator for 4 days or frozen for several months.

PER SERVING Calories: 476, Protein: 11g, Total Carbohydrates: 34g, Fiber: 6g, Total Fat: 29g, Saturated Fat: 4g, Cholesterol: 0mg, Sodium: 1480mg

Roasted Cauliflower with Saffron Dipping Sauce

Serves 4   Prep time: 10 minutes   Cook time: 15 minutes

QUICK & EASY | VEGETARIAN | GLUTEN-FREE   Roasting cauliflower makes it crunchy and gives it a sweet, mildly nutty flavor. It's a good way to get someone who doesn't like vegetables to eat a vegetable! The saffron sauce is made from yogurt and helps cool the heat from the hot smoked paprika. If you can't find smoked hot paprika, substitute chipotle powder. Saffron is the stigma from a particular variety of crocus. It's native to the Mediterranean, and most imported saffron comes from Spain.

FOR THE CAULIFLOWER
¼ cup extra-virgin olive oil
2 teaspoons salt
1 teaspoon smoked hot paprika
   (or chipotle powder)
1 head cauliflower, stem trimmed,
   cut into florets
½ lemon

FOR THE SAFFRON SAUCE
¼ teaspoon saffron threads
1 tablespoon water
1 cup Greek yogurt
1 teaspoon salt
½ teaspoon ground turmeric
1 scallion, finely chopped
1 tablespoon chopped fresh cilantro

✳ This dish can be made ahead, and the cauliflower can be served either hot or at room temperature. If you make it ahead and want to serve it warm, crisp the cauliflower in a hot oven before serving.

MAKE THE CAULIFLOWER

1. Preheat the oven to 400°F.

2. In a large bowl, combine the olive oil, salt, and paprika or chipotle powder. Add the cauliflower and mix well until it is evenly coated.

3. Arrange the cauliflower in a single layer on a rimmed baking sheet (you may need two baking sheets).

4. Roast until the cauliflower is brown around the edges, about 15 minutes, stirring occasionally.

5. Squeeze the lemon juice over the cauliflower.

MAKE THE SAFFRON SAUCE

1. In a small bowl or saucer, combine the saffron threads with the water. This releases the color and flavor.

2. In a small bowl, combine the yogurt, saffron-water mixture, salt, turmeric, scallion, and cilantro. Mix well.

3. Arrange the cauliflower on a serving dish along with a bowl of saffron dip, and serve.

4. The cooked cauliflower will keep 5 days in the refrigerator, and the sauce will keep 4 days in the refrigerator.

PER SERVING Calories: 171, Protein: 5g, Total Carbohydrates: 8g, Fiber: 2g, Total Fat: 13g, Saturated Fat: 2g, Cholesterol: 4mg, Sodium: 1808mg

Sautéed Almonds with Apricots

Serves 4   Prep time: 10 minutes   Cook time: 5 minutes

QUICK & EASY | VEGAN | GLUTEN-FREE   Almonds sautéed in olive oil, sprinkled with sea salt, and served with bits of dried apricots are a great snack any time, but my favorite time to eat this is with a crisp white wine while cooking dinner. You can substitute unsalted pistachios or walnuts for the almonds in this recipe.

2 tablespoons extra-virgin olive oil

1 cup blanched (skinless) unsalted almonds

½ teaspoon sea salt

⅛ teaspoon red pepper flakes (optional)

⅛ teaspoon ground cinnamon

½ cup dried apricots, chopped

❋ My favorite salt to use in this recipe is fleur de sel, the classic sea salt of Europe. It's a hand-harvested sea salt collected from the top layer of salt evaporated in in large salt pans. It has large grains and a very complex flavor because it is completely unprocessed and contains a lot of minerals. If you can't get fleur de sel, substitute any high-quality sea salt or kosher salt.

1. Place a medium frying pan over high heat. Add the olive oil, almonds, and sea salt and sauté until the almonds are a light golden brown, 5 to 10 minutes. It's important to stir constantly while cooking them since they burn easily.

2. Spoon the hot almonds into a serving dish and add the red pepper flakes (if using), cinnamon, and apricot pieces.

3. Let cool and serve.

4. These nuts can be stored in an airtight container at room temperature 4 or 5 days.

PER SERVING Calories: 207, Protein: 5g, Total Carbohydrates: 7g, Fiber: 3g, Total Fat: 19g, Saturated Fat: 2g, Cholesterol: 0mg, Sodium: 235mg

Melon Granita

Serves 4 to 6   Prep time: 10 minutes, plus 3 hours to freeze

VEGAN | GLUTEN-FREE | BIG 8 ALLERGEN-FRIENDLY   In the hot summer heat of the Middle East and the Mediterranean, refreshing fruit ices are served everywhere. In my traveling 20s, I would seek out any restaurant that served granita. The hot climate also creates intensely sweet and flavorful melons. Granitas are very easy to make. You will want to allow at lest 3 hours for it to freeze, or you can just make it the day before you intend to serve it.

½ cup sugar
½ cup water
1 ripe honeydew or other melon, peeled, seeded, and cut into 1-inch pieces
1 tablespoon lemon or lime juice
2 teaspoons finely chopped fresh mint

❋ You can make granita 1 day ahead, cover it, and keep in the freezer until ready to serve. Shortly before serving, break up and fluff the granita again with a fork.

1. Place the sugar and water in a small saucepan over medium heat. Stir until the sugar dissolves. Set aside and allow to cool completely.

2. When the sugar syrup has cooled, place it in a food processor or blender with the melon, lemon or lime juice, and mint. Process until smooth.

3. Pour the melon mixture into a 9-by-13-inch freezer-safe dish and place on a level spot in the freezer.

4. After 1 hour, break up the mixture with a fork. It will be frozen around the edges and slushy in the middle.

5. Every 30 minutes, remove the granita and break up the ice crystals with a fork. Granita should be light and fluffy and icy.

6. Spoon the granita into serving dishes and serve immediately.

7. Granita should be eaten within 48 hours of being made, because it gets too icy if stored longer.

PER SERVING Calories: 211, Protein: 1g, Total Carbohydrates: 54g, Fiber: 3g, Total Fat: 0g, Saturated Fat: 0g, Cholesterol: 0mg, Sodium: 58mg

Balsamic-Roasted Figs with Goat Cheese

Serves 4   Prep time: 15 minutes   Cook time: 15 minutes

QUICK & EASY | VEGETARIAN | GLUTEN-FREE   I still resent buying figs at the market. As a kid growing up in Oakland California, there were fig trees all over my neighborhood. All us kids would harvest them and either eat them whole or pull them apart and suck the soft fruit off the skin. This recipe is far more sophisticated than my childhood fig eating days, and I love it.

2 tablespoons butter, melted

1 tablespoon extra-virgin olive oil

12 fresh figs, stems removed, cut in half

½ cup honey

1 tablespoon balsamic vinegar

½ teaspoon ground cinnamon

4 sprigs fresh rosemary

⅛ teaspoon salt

½ pound chèvre

½ cup crushed almond biscotti or other almond cookie (not made with wheat flour)

✳ This dish uses fresh figs, which are typically available in late summer and early fall. If you can't find fresh, substitute dried figs but soak them in boiling water 30 minutes before using them in this recipe. You can also make this recipe with fresh strawberries or pitted plums.

1. Preheat the oven to 375°F.

2. In a medium bowl, combine the butter, olive oil, figs, honey, vinegar, cinnamon, rosemary, and salt. Gently mix and pour the mixture into a 9-by-13-inch baking dish.

3. Bake the figs 10 to 15 minutes or until they begin to wrinkle.

4. Cut the chèvre into four equal pieces and place one piece of chèvre in each serving dish.

5. Remove the rosemary sprigs. Spoon the roasted fruit over the chèvre and top with a garnish of crushed biscotti. Serve warm or at room temperature.

6. The roasted fruit can be stored in the refrigerator for 5 days. For the best flavor, let the fruit sit for 30 minutes at room temperature before assembling the dessert.

PER SERVING Calories: 532, Protein: 14g, Total Carbohydrates: 77g, Fiber: 6g, Total Fat: 23g, Saturated Fat: 12g, Cholesterol: 60mg, Sodium: 217mg

Yogurt Cheese with Berries

Serves 4   Prep time: 15 minutes, plus overnight to drain

VEGETARIAN | GLUTEN-FREE   Yogurt cheese is simply yogurt that has been strained overnight so much of the liquid drains off, leaving behind thick, rich yogurt that has the consistency of cream cheese. We used to spread it on toast with jam (in fact, we still do), or you can serve it as a dessert with berries. You can mix it with herbs and onions for a savory spread. You'll need a piece of cheesecloth folded into a triple thickness and a fine-mesh strainer to make yogurt cheese.

1½ quarts (6 cups) plain yogurt

3 cups mixed fresh berries

3 tablespoons honey

1 tablespoon balsamic vinegar

¼ cup toasted slivered
    unsalted almonds

✳ If you like tart yogurt cheese, let the yogurt drain for 2 hours at room temperature and then place it in the refrigerator overnight.

1. Line the cheesecloth in the mesh strainer, making sure there is plenty of cheesecloth hanging over the sides of the strainer.

2. Carefully spoon the yogurt into the strainer. Do not stir it.

3. Fold the cheesecloth over the yogurt and place the strainer in a larger bowl. Refrigerate overnight.

4. The next day, remove the top layer of cheesecloth and invert the yogurt cheese onto a serving plate. Remove the rest of the cheesecloth and discard.

5. In a medium bowl, combine the berries, honey, and balsamic vinegar. Slightly mash the berries to release the juices.

6. Spoon the berries over the yogurt cheese, top with toasted almonds, and serve. You can serve it either sliced in wedges or spooned into serving plates.

7. Yogurt cheese will keep about 1 week in the refrigerator.

PER SERVING Calories: 379, Protein: 23g, Total Carbohydrates: 48g, Fiber: 3g, Total Fat: 8g, Saturated Fat: 4g, Cholesterol: 22mg, Sodium: 259mg

Yogurt, Date, and Walnut Parfait

Serves 4   Prep time: 15 minutes

QUICK & EASY | VEGETARIAN | GLUTEN-FREE   Layers of Greek yogurt, dates, honey, and toasted walnuts sprinkled with cinnamon on top—what could be easier? I like serving this light and creamy dessert after a hearty dinner of stew or couscous.

1 quart (4 cups) plain Greek yogurt
8 pitted dates, chopped
½ cup finely chopped toasted walnuts
½ cup honey
1 teaspoon ground cinnamon

❋ If not you're not serving the parfaits right away, it's best to wait and add the cinnamon before serving. These parfaits can be made several hours before serving, but don't chill them too long or the nuts will lose their crunch.

1. Place a spoonful of yogurt in the bottom of each of four parfait or champagne glasses.

2. Top with a layer of dates, a sprinkling of walnuts, and a drizzle of honey.

3. Add another layer of yogurt, top with another layer of dates, walnuts, and honey, and finish with one last layer of honey.

4. Dust each parfait with cinnamon. Place in the refrigerator until you're ready to serve.

PER SERVING Calories: 448, Protein: 18g, Total Carbohydrates: 67g, Fiber: 3g, Total Fat: 12g, Saturated Fat: 3g, Cholesterol: 15mg, Sodium: 174mg

Apricot Walnut Cake

Serves 6   Prep time: 15 minutes   Cook time: 35 minutes

VEGETARIAN | GLUTEN-FREE   This moist pudding-like cake is made with olive oil instead of butter and studded with plump apricots. It's best served warm with a dollop of whipped cream or yogurt. The recipe calls for frozen apricots, but of course, if they're in season, use fresh.

⅓ cup extra-virgin olive oil, divided

3 eggs

1 cup sugar

1¼ cups finely chopped walnuts

2 tablespoons rice flour

2 teaspoons pure vanilla extract

1 (10-ounce) package frozen apricot halves, thawed

✳ If you don't like the taste of olive oil, you can use an equal amount of melted, cooled butter in this recipe. You can substitute unsalted almonds for walnuts, and use any stone fruit or berry, fresh or frozen.

1. Preheat the oven to 375°F.

2. Brush a 9-inch pie plate with 1 tablespoon olive oil and set aside.

3. In a blender or food processor, combine the remaining olive oil, eggs, sugar, walnuts, rice flour, and vanilla. Process until smooth.

4. Arrange the apricots in the oiled pie plate. Pour the walnut batter over the apricots and bake for 35 to 45 minutes, or until the cake is golden brown.

5. Let the cake sit for 10 minutes before serving. Spoon it into serving dishes while it is still warm or cut it into wedges at room temperature.

6. This dish keeps 5 days in the refrigerator or several months in the freezer.

PER SERVING Calories: 442, Protein: 10g, Total Carbohydrates: 42g, Fiber: 2g, Total Fat: 29g, Saturated Fat: 3g, Cholesterol: 82mg, Sodium: 32mg

Cherry Clafoutis

Serves 4 to 6   Prep time: 10 minutes   Cook time: 35 minutes

VEGETARIAN   Clafoutis is fruit that is baked in batter. It's served throughout France for breakfast or dessert. A clafoutis is the forebearer of an American cobbler. I'm using cherries in this recipe, but any berry or stone fruit works well. You can use fresh or frozen berries. If you're using frozen, let them thaw before making the dessert.

2 tablespoons butter, at room temperature

½ cup ground unsalted almonds

1¼ cups milk

½ cup sugar, divided

2 eggs

1 tablespoon pure vanilla extract

½ cup all-purpose flour

⅛ teaspoon salt

3 cups pitted cherries

❋ You can make clafoutis ahead of time and rewarm it or allow to come to room temperature before serving. To make a gluten-free clafoutis, substitute an equal amount of coconut or rice flour for the wheat flour.

1. Preheat the oven to 350°F.

2. Brush a 9-inch pie plate with the butter and sprinkle with the ground almonds.

3. In a blender or food processor, combine the milk, ¼ cup sugar, eggs, vanilla, flour, and salt, and purée until smooth.

4. Pour the batter into the prepared pie plate. Arrange the cherries over the batter and sprinkle with the remaining ¼ cup sugar.

5. Bake 35 to 45 minutes, or until the clafoutis is golden brown.

6. Let cool at least 10 minutes before serving.

PER SERVING Calories: 407, Protein: 10g, Total Carbohydrates: 57g, Fiber: 4g, Total Fat: 16g, Saturated Fat: 6g, Cholesterol: 103mg, Sodium: 182mg

Chocolate Olive Oil Brownies

Serves 12   Prep time: 15 minutes   Cook time: 35 minutes

VEGETARIAN   Who doesn't love a brownie? But with olive oil? Chocolate and olive oil are surprisingly good together. The olive oil makes the brownies rich and fudgy. With the healthy fats in olive oil and the antioxidants in chocolate, you can pretend this is health food!

¼ cup extra-virgin olive oil,
    plus 1 tablespoon to oil the pan
¾ cup sugar
1 egg
2 teaspoons pure vanilla extract
8 ounces bittersweet chocolate,
    melted and cooled
½ cup all-purpose flour
¼ cup cocoa powder
½ teaspoon fleur de sel (or kosher salt)

✻ Chocolate should be melted gently. You can either melt it over hot, barely simmering water in a double boiler, or you can melt it in the microwave. If you do it in the microwave, go very slowly and err on the side of too little time rather than too much. The amount of time and power of the microwave varies greatly depending on the manufacturer.

1. Preheat the oven to 375°F.

2. Brush an 8-inch pan with 1 tablespoon olive oil and set aside.

3. Combine ¼ cup olive oil, the sugar, egg, and vanilla in a medium bowl and beat on high until light and fluffy, about 3 to 5 minutes.

4. Fold in the chocolate, flour, and cocoa powder.

5. Spoon the batter into the prepared pan, sprinkle the top with fleur de sel, and bake for 35 to 45 minutes, or until a toothpick inserted in the middle comes out clean.

6. Remove from the oven and allow the brownies to cool completely before cutting.

7. These brownies can be stored in an airtight container at room temperature for 5 days or frozen for several months.

PER SERVING Calories: 214, Protein: 3g, Total Carbohydrates: 29g, Fiber: 1g, Total Fat: 11g, Saturated Fat: 5g, Cholesterol: 18mg, Sodium: 117mg

Pistachio Almond Baklava

Serves 12   Prep time: 40 minutes   Cook time: 35 minutes

VEGETARIAN   Phyllo is a paper-thin pastry used throughout the Middle East and is sold in the freezer section of most grocery stores (typically next to the frozen pie crusts). Phyllo dries quickly and becomes crumbly and unusable if it gets too dry, so it's best to have everything ready and assemble the baklava as quickly as you can. You can use any nuts you'd like, but I really like the buttery, almost cherry-like flavor of pistachios and almonds.

½ cup honey
1 cup sugar, divided
½ cup water
3 cups finely chopped unsalted almonds
1 cup finely chopped unsalted pistachios
1 teaspoon cinnamon
½ pound butter, melted
1 (16-ounce) package phyllo, thawed

❋ You score the top of the baklava to keep it from cracking, but those score lines also make a guide of where to cut it when cooled. You can easily cut this recipe into 24 pieces if you are serving a crowd.

1. Preheat the oven to 375°F.

2. Place the honey, ½ cup sugar, and the water in a medium pot over medium heat. Stir to dissolve the sugar. When it has dissolved, increase the heat to high and bring to a boil. Reduce to a simmer and cook about 5 minutes. Set aside.

3. In a medium bowl, combine the almonds, pistachios, ½ cup sugar, and the cinnamon. Mix well.

4. Brush a 9-by-13-inch pan with butter.

5. Unwrap the phyllo and place it on a cookie sheet. Cover it with a piece of plastic wrap.

6. Place a sheet of phyllo in the buttered pan and cover the rest with the plastic wrap. Butter the sheet in the pan using a pastry brush, and top it with another sheet of phyllo.

7. Layer six sheets of phyllo in the pan, buttering between each sheet. Top with half the nut mixture.

8. Top with another six sheets of phyllo, buttering between each sheet, and top with the remaining nut mixture. Top with the remaining phyllo, buttering in between each layer.

9. Score the top layer of phyllo into 12 pieces. Bake 35 to 45 minutes or until the phyllo is golden brown.

10. When the baklava has cooked, gently pour the honey-sugar syrup all over the pastry. Let the baklava sit at room temperature until completely cool before serving. Serve at room temperature.

11. Baklava can be kept at room temperature in an airtight container for 1 week. It should not be refrigerated because it will get soggy.

PER SERVING Calories: 434, Protein: 7g, Total Carbohydrates: 40g, Fiber: 4g, Total Fat: 30g, Saturated Fat: 11g, Cholesterol: 41mg, Sodium: 172mg

twelve

Stocks, Sauces & Condiments

Slow Cooker Vegetable Stock

Makes 6 cups   Prep time: 10 minutes   Cook time: 6 hours

QUICK & EASY | VEGAN | GLUTEN-FREE | BIG 8 ALLERGEN-FREE   Every great cook deserves to start with homemade stock or broth, and with a slow cooker it's a breeze. The rule of stock is to use aromatic and root vegetables, typically onions, carrots, and celery, but feel free to experiment and create your own "house" favorite.

2 leeks, root and top trimmed,
   cut in half lengthwise
1 fennel bulb, cut in half
1 onion, cut in half
2 carrots, peeled and cut into
   2-inch pieces
1 head garlic, cut in half across
   the middle
4 sprigs fresh flatleaf parsley
1 sprig fresh rosemary
6 cups water

❋ To make beef or chicken stock, add 2 pounds of chicken or beef bones or a mixture of the two. For a more deeply flavored stock, you can roast the vegetables and bones before placing them in the slow cooker.

1. Place the leeks, fennel, onion, carrots, garlic, parsley, rosemary, and water in a slow cooker, cover, and cook on low for 6 hours.

2. Use a slotted spoon to remove all the vegetables.

3. Pour the remaining stock through a strainer set over a large bowl.

4. Pour the strained stock into jars or plastic containers to store.

5. Stock will last 1 week in the refrigerator or for several months in the freezer. Freeze it in 1- or 2-cup containers for easy thawing.

PER SERVING Calories: 20, Protein: 1g, Total Carbohydrates: 4g, Fiber: 1g, Total Fat: 0g, Saturated Fat: 0g, Cholesterol: 0mg, Sodium: 78mg

Olive Oil Mayonnaise

Makes about 1½ cups   Prep time: 15 minutes

QUICK & EASY | VEGETARIAN | GLUTEN-FREE   Why make your own mayonnaise? Because most commercial mayonnaises aren't made with healthy oils and have added sugars. Homemade mayonnaise is easy if you have a food processor or immersion blender, but very difficult if you're making it by hand with a whisk.

1 egg yolk
1 tablespoon lemon juice
1 teaspoon Dijon mustard
1 teaspoon salt
¼ teaspoon freshly ground
    black pepper
1 cup extra-virgin olive oil

❋ If you don't have a food processor, you can make this in a blender or use an immersion blender. With a blender, just follow the recipe. With an immersion blender, its easier to add 2 tablespoons of olive oil at a time, blending slightly before adding more olive oil rather than trying to manipulate the immersion blender while you're adding the oil.

1. In the bowl of a food processor, combine the egg yolk, lemon juice, mustard, salt, and pepper.

2. With the machine running, slowly drizzle the olive oil into the egg mixture. The mixture will become thick and creamy. If the mayonnaise is too thick, thin it with a bit of water.

3. Spoon it into a jar with a tightly fitting lid and store it in the refrigerator.

4. Mayonnaise can last for 7 days in the refrigerator.

PER SERVING Calories: 75, Protein: 0g, Total Carbohydrates: 0g, Fiber: 0g, Total Fat: 9g, Saturated Fat: 1g, Cholesterol: 9mg, Sodium: 100mg

Aioli

Makes about 1 ½ cups   Prep time: 15 minutes

QUICK & EASY | VEGETARIAN | GLUTEN-FREE   Aioli is simply mayonnaise with garlic added. The garlic should be puréed before making the sauce so it's as smooth as possible. Aioli is delicious on just about anything–roasted potatoes, raw vegetables, seafood, steamed asparagus, boiled artichokes, or slathered on sandwiches instead of mayonnaise.

2 garlic cloves, peeled and crushed

1 teaspoon salt, divided

1 egg yolk

1 tablespoon lemon juice

½ teaspoon Dijon mustard

¼ teaspoon freshly ground
   black pepper

1 cup extra-virgin olive oil

3 tablespoons water

❋ In a hurry and need an aioli cheat? Mix 1 or 2 cloves of minced garlic and 1 tablespoon of olive oil into a cup of prepared mayonnaise.

1. Place the garlic cloves on a cutting board, sprinkle with ½ teaspoon salt, and mash with the back of a spoon until the garlic is puréed.

2. In the bowl of a food processor, combine the garlic purée, egg yolk, lemon juice, mustard, remaining ½ teaspoon salt, and pepper.

3. With the machine running, slowly drizzle the olive oil into the egg mixture. The mixture will become thick and creamy. When all the olive oil has been added, add the water a little bit at a time.

4. Spoon it into a jar with a tightly fitting lid and store it in the refrigerator.

5. Aioli can keep 5 days in the refrigerator.

PER SERVING Calories: 75, Protein: 0g, Total Carbohydrates: 0g, Fiber: 0g, Total Fat: 9g, Saturated Fat: 1g, Cholesterol: 9mg, Sodium: 99mg

Hummus

Serves 4 to 6   Prep time: 10 minutes

QUICK & EASY | VEGAN | GLUTEN-FREE | BIG 8 ALLERGEN-FRIENDLY   Who doesn't love hummus? It's a snap to prepare and provides a high-protein nutritious snack. It can be made ahead and lasts about 1 week, making it just about the perfect food to have on hand. Serve it with fresh vegetables or Toasted Pita Wedges with Sea Salt (page 186). This hummus is mild, with only one garlic clove, but feel free to add more garlic or ½ cup fire-roasted red peppers. Walnut oil is a delicious substitute for olive oil in this recipe.

1 (15-ounce) can garbanzo beans, drained and rinsed

1 garlic clove, crushed

½ cup tahini

¼ cup extra-virgin olive oil, plus more for drizzling

3 tablespoons lemon juice

1½ teaspoons salt

½ teaspoon paprika

¼ teaspoon freshly ground black pepper

1 tablespoon chopped fresh flatleaf parsley

❋ You can make hummus in a blender, but because of the way the blender jar is shaped, it's hard to get the beans to purée evenly, so add ¼ cup water to help it along.

1. In a food processor, combine the beans, garlic, tahini, olive oil, lemon juice, salt, paprika, and pepper. Process until smooth. If the mixture is too thick, thin it with water, 1 tablespoon at a time.

2. Spoon the hummus into a serving bowl, garnish with parsley, and drizzle with oil.

3. Hummus keeps about 1 week in the refrigerator.

PER SERVING Calories: 412, Protein: 12g, Total Carbohydrates: 22g, Fiber: 7g, Total Fat: 31g, Saturated Fat: 4g, Cholesterol: 10mg, Sodium: 910mg

Tapenade

Makes about 1½ cups   Prep time: 15 minutes

QUICK & EASY | VEGAN | GLUTEN-FREE | BIG 8 ALLERGEN-FRIENDLY   Tapenade is a chopped olive condiment that adds a burst of flavor to any dish. It pairs well with white fish and lamb. Stir a little into mayonnaise for an unbelievably delicious sandwich spread. You can make it with any kind of pitted olives, black or green, or a combination of both.

1 cup pitted Kalamata olives

1 garlic clove, minced

2 tablespoons lemon juice

1 tablespoon chopped fresh
    flatleaf parsley

¼ cup extra-virgin olive oil

¼ teaspoon salt

¼ teaspoon freshly ground
    black pepper

❋ If you don't have a food processor and don't mind a chunkier tapenade, chop the olives as finely as you can and combine with the remaining ingredients.

1. Place the olives, garlic, lemon juice, parsley, olive oil, salt, and pepper in the bowl of a food processor and pulse several times until the mixture is well blended but still has texture.

2. Spoon the tapenade into a jar with a tightly fitting lid and store it in the refrigerator.

3. Tapenade will keep 2 weeks in the refrigerator.

PER SERVING Calories: 50, Protein: 0g, Total Carbohydrates: 0g, Fiber: 0g, Total Fat: 6g, Saturated Fat: 0g, Cholesterol: 0mg, Sodium: 144mg

Pesto

Makes about 1½ cups   Prep time: 15 minutes

QUICK & EASY | VEGETARIAN | GLUTEN-FREE   It's best to make pesto when basil is in season and is reasonably priced, because it freezes well. This recipe uses walnuts, but pesto can be made with almonds, pine nuts, or a mixture of nuts.

2 cups packed fresh basil leaves

½ cup toasted walnuts, finely chopped

½ cup extra-virgin olive oil

1 clove garlic, crushed

½ cup grated Parmesan cheese

2 tablespoons lemon juice

1 teaspoon salt

¼ teaspoon freshly ground
   black pepper

※ Traditional pesto is made with basil, but you can experiment with other herbs, especially if you have an abundance of them growing in your garden. You can use an equal amount of mint, cilantro, or parsley to basil, but if you're using stronger herbs like thyme, oregano, or rosemary, ½ cup will be plenty for the whole recipe.

1. Combine basil, walnuts, olive oil, garlic, Parmesan cheese, lemon juice, salt, and pepper in the bowl of a food processor and process until smooth.

2. Spoon the pesto into a container and store it in the refrigerator or freezer until ready to use.

3. Pesto can be stored in the refrigerator for 10 days or frozen for about 8 months. If freezing pesto, it's best to store it in small containers for easy use.

PER SERVING Calories: 61, Protein: 2g, Total Carbohydrates: 1g, Fiber: 0g, Total Fat: 6g, Saturated Fat: 1g, Cholesterol: 2mg, Sodium: 119mg

Tzatziki

Makes about 2 cups   Prep time: 15 minutes

QUICK & EASY | VEGETARIAN | GLUTEN-FREE   Known by many names–*raita* in Indian cooking and *cucumber dill sauce* in the Western world–tzatziki is enjoyed as a sauce and condiment throughout the Middle East. It should be thick, rich, creamy, and refreshing. Using Greek yogurt makes all the difference in this recipe.

1 English cucumber, peeled, seeded, and finely chopped

2 teaspoons salt, divided

1½ cups plain Greek yogurt

1 garlic clove, minced

2 tablespoons lemon juice

2 teaspoons chopped fresh dill

¼ teaspoon freshly ground black pepper

Olive oil, for drizzling

❋ If you are unable to find Greek yogurt, you can either follow the technique for making Yogurt Cheese (page 195) or you can use a 50-50 mixture of yogurt and sour cream. You can also substitute the dill with chopped fresh mint for a cooler taste.

1. Toss the cucumber with 1 teaspoon salt and place in a strainer to drain for about 20 minutes. Blot any remaining water off with a paper towel.

2. In a medium bowl, combine the yogurt, garlic, lemon juice, dill, 1 teaspoon salt, the pepper, and the drained cucumbers. Stir to combine. Don't overmix or the mixture will become runny.

3. Spoon the tzatziki into a serving dish and drizzle with olive oil.

4. Tzatziki can be stored in the refrigerator for 5 days.

PER SERVING Calories: 41, Protein: 3g, Total Carbohydrates: 5g, Fiber: 0g, Total Fat: 1g, Saturated Fat: 1g, Cholesterol: 3mg, Sodium: 616mg

Apricot Balsamic Dressing

Makes about 1½ cups   Prep time: 15 minutes

QUICK & EASY | VEGAN | GLUTEN-FREE | BIG 8 ALLERGEN-FREE   This sweet-and-sour dressing is delicious served over bitter greens—radicchio and endive—that are loved throughout Europe and the Mediterranean. It pairs wonderfully with goat cheese and feta and is delicious on chicken and pork.

5 dried apricots, chopped
½ cup boiling water
⅔ cup extra-virgin olive oil
1 shallot, chopped
2 tablespoons balsamic vinegar
1 tablespoon lemon juice
1 teaspoon Dijon mustard
1 teaspoon salt
¼ teaspoon freshly ground
   black pepper
⅛ teaspoon red pepper flakes
   (optional)

❋ This recipe uses dried apricots but can be made with an equal amount of fresh or thawed frozen apricots instead. If using fresh or thawed, there's no need to soak them in boiling water, so skip step 1.

1. Combine the apricots with the boiling water and let them sit for 15 minutes to soften. Drain.

2. In a blender or food processor, combine the drained apricots, olive oil, shallot, balsamic vinegar, lemon juice, mustard, salt, pepper, and red pepper flakes (if using). Process until smooth.

3. Store in the refrigerator until ready to use. This dressing will keep 10 days in the refrigerator.

PER SERVING Calories: 103, Protein: 0g, Total Carbohydrates: 2g, Fiber: 0g, Total Fat: 11g, Saturated Fat: 2g, Cholesterol: 0mg, Sodium: 199mg

Feta, Yogurt, and Dill Dressing

Makes about 1½ cups   Prep time: 15 minutes

QUICK & EASY | VEGETARIAN | GLUTEN-FREE   Use this creamy dressing instead of blue cheese dressing in some of your favorite salads, or as a sauce over roasted vegetables, chicken, or salmon.

1 cup plain Greek yogurt

2 ounces feta cheese, crumbled

¼ cup extra-virgin olive oil

2 scallions, chopped

1 tablespoon lemon juice

1 tablespoon honey

1 teaspoon chopped fresh dill

1 teaspoon salt

¼ teaspoon freshly ground
   black pepper

❋ You can substitute crumbled goat cheese instead of feta, or leave out the cheese entirely.

1. In a small bowl, combine the yogurt, feta, olive oil, scallions, lemon juice, honey, dill, salt, and pepper. Mix well.

2. Store in the refrigerator until ready to use. This dressing will keep 5 days in the refrigerator.

PER SERVING Calories: 70, Protein: 2g, Total Carbohydrates: 3g, Fiber: 0g, Total Fat: 6g, Saturated Fat: 2g, Cholesterol: 5mg, Sodium: 262mg

Pickled Beets

Makes about 1 cup   Prep time: 15 minutes

QUICK & EASY | VEGAN | GLUTEN-FREE | BIG 8 ALLERGEN-FRIENDLY   Pickled vegetables are a way to use up nature's bounty or extend the shelf life of vegetables with a short season. Sweet beets are easy to pickle and can be eaten within 30 minutes of pickling. However, the longer the beets can sit in the pickling juices, the better the flavor. You can add any flavorings you like to the beets. I'm using garlic, peppercorns, and thyme here. Splash some of the pickling juice on your salad instead of vinegar, or remove the peppercorns and thyme sprigs to turn the pickled beets themselves into a salad. For a delicious variation, add ½ cup finely chopped red onions and 1 tablespoon of chopped mint to the recipe. A dollop of yogurt can also be added as a creamy, tangy topping.

1 bunch beets, peeled and cut
   into ½-inch pieces
2 teaspoons salt
1 teaspoon sugar
¾ cup red wine vinegar
6 whole peppercorns
1 clove garlic, sliced
4 sprigs fresh thyme

❀ You can make this recipe with golden beets. Use white wine vinegar or apple cider vinegar instead of red wine vinegar to retain the beets' beautiful golden color.

1. Place the beets in a medium saucepan. Cover with water, add 1 teaspoon salt, and bring to a boil. Cook 5 to 10 minutes, or until beets are tender. Drain.

2. In a glass container where you are going to store the beets, add the sugar, remaining salt, and vinegar. Cover and shake until the sugar dissolves.

3. Add the beets, peppercorns, garlic, and thyme. Cover and set aside room temperature for at least 30 minutes before serving.

4. After 30 minutes, store the pickled beets in the refrigerator for up to 1 month.

PER SERVING (¼ cup) Calories: 69, Protein: 2g, Total Carbohydrates: 14g, Fiber: 3g, Total Fat: 0g, Saturated Fat: 0g, Cholesterol: 0mg, Sodium: 413mg

Acknowledgments

I was born into a large Greek family filled with good cooks and fabulous farmers who ensured we always had something delicious and healthy to eat. My childhood experiences fostered a deep respect for food and cooking, which has sustained me both professionally and personally my entire life. I'd like to thank my family for setting me off on the right path.

Additionally, I'd like to thank my husband, Bob, my daughter, Claire, and all my friends and family who gather around my table. Lastly, I'd like to thank my editor, Clara Song Lee, for her good humor and grace, and the entire Callisto Media team.

The Dirty Dozen
& The Clean Fifteen

2016

DIRTY DOZEN	CLEAN FIFTEEN
Apples	Asparagus
Celery	Avocados
Cherries	Cabbage
Cherry tomatoes	Cantaloupe
Cucumbers	Cauliflower
Grapes	Corn
Nectarines	Eggplant
Peaches	Grapefruit
Spinach	Honeydew melon
Strawberries	Kiwis
Sweet bell peppers	Mangoes
Tomatoes	Onions
	Papayas
	Pineapples
	Sweet peas (frozen)

In addition to the Dirty Dozen, the EWG added two foods contaminated with highly toxic organophosphate insecticides:

Hot peppers

Kale/Collard greens

A nonprofit and environmental watchdog organization called Environmental Working Group (EWG) looks at data supplied by the US Department of Agriculture (USDA) and the Food and Drug Administration (FDA) about pesticide residues. Each year it compiles a list of the best and worst pesticide loads found in commercial crops. You can use these lists to decide which fruits and vegetables to buy organic to minimize your exposure to pesticides and which produce is considered safe enough to buy conventionally. This does not mean that the Clean Fifteen produce is pesticide-free, though, so wash these fruits and vegetables thoroughly. These lists change every year, so make sure you look up the most recent before you fill your shopping cart. You'll find the most recent lists as well as a guide to pesticides in produce at EWG.org/FoodNews.

Measurements & Conversions

VOLUME EQUIVALENTS (LIQUID)

US STANDARD	US STANDARD (OUNCES)	METRIC (APPROXIMATE)
2 tablespoons	1 fl. oz.	30 mL
¼ cup	2 fl. oz.	60 mL
½ cup	4 fl. oz.	120 mL
1 cup	8 fl. oz.	240 mL
1½ cups	12 fl. oz.	355 mL
2 cups or 1 pint	16 fl. oz.	475 mL
4 cups or 1 quart	32 fl. oz.	1 L
1 gallon	128 fl. oz.	4 L

OVEN TEMPERATURES

FAHRENHEIT (F)	CELSIUS (C) (APPROXIMATE)
250	120
300	150
325	165
350	180
375	190
400	200
425	220
450	230

VOLUME EQUIVALENTS (DRY)

US STANDARD	METRIC (APPROXIMATE)
⅛ teaspoon	0.5 mL
¼ teaspoon	1 mL
½ teaspoon	2 mL
¾ teaspoon	4 mL
1 teaspoon	5 mL
1 tablespoon	15 mL
¼ cup	59 mL
⅓ cup	79 mL
½ cup	118 mL
⅔ cup	156 mL
¾ cup	177 mL
1 cup	235 mL
2 cups or 1 pint	475 mL
3 cups	700 mL
4 cups or 1 quart	1 L
½ gallon	2 L
1 gallon	4 L

WEIGHT EQUIVALENTS

US STANDARD	METRIC (APPROXIMATE)
½ ounce	15 g
1 ounce	30 g
2 ounces	60 g
4 ounces	115 g
8 ounces	225 g
12 ounces	340 g
16 ounces or 1 pound	455 g

References

Buettner, Dan. *The Blue Zones Solution: Eating and Living Like the World's Healthiest People.* Washington, DC: National Geographic, 2015.

Clinical Nutrition Services Department, University of Wisconsin-Madison. "Health Facts for You: Mediterranean Diet Food Guide." Accessed March 24, 2016. www.uhs.wisc.edu /health-topics/healthy-lifestyle/documents /Mediterranean.pdf.

Harvard School of Public Health, Oldways Preservation Trust, World Health Organization. "1993 International Conference on the Diets of the Mediterranean." Cambridge, MA.

Keys, Ancel, and Margaret Keys. *How to Eat Well and Stay Well the Mediterranean Way.* New York: Doubleday, 1975.

Oldways Preservation Trust. "Mediterranean Diet Pyramid." Accessed March 24, 2016. oldwayspt.org/resources/heritage-pyramids /mediterranean-pyramid/overview.

Samieri, Cécilia, et al. "The Association between Dietary Patterns at Midlife and Health in Aging: An Observational Study." *Annals of Internal Medicine* 159 no. 9 (2013): 584-591.

Seven Countries Study. "Cross-Cultural Findings of the Seven Countries Study." Accessed March 24, 2016. sevencountriesstudy.com/study -findings/cross-cultural.

US Department of Health and Human Services. "A Healthy Mediterranean-Style Eating Pattern." Accessed March 24, 2016. health.gov/dietary guidelines/2015/guidelines/appendix-4/.

Resources

BOOKS

Acquista, Angelo. *The Mediterranean Prescription: Meal Plans and Recipes to Help You Stay Slim and Healthy for the Rest of Your Life.* New York: Ballantine Books, 2006.

The Mediterranean Diet for Beginners: The Complete Guide–40 Delicious Recipes, 7-Day Diet Meal Plan, and 10 Tips for Success. Berkeley, CA: Rockridge Press, 2013.

Ozner, Michael. *The Complete Mediterranean Diet: Everything You Need to Know to Lose Weight and Lower Your Risk of Heart Disease.* Dallas: BenBella Books, 2014.

ONLINE INFORMATION

Environmental Working Group
ewg.org/research/ewgs-good-seafood-guide

The Environmental Working Group lists seafood that is low in mercury, high in omega-3s, and sustainable.

Monterey Bay Aquarium Seafood Watch
seafoodwatch.org/seafood-recommendations/consumer-guides

These lists of fish that are farmed or caught in the most sustainable way are downloadable for every state.

Oldways
oldwayspt.org

A nonprofit food and nutrition education organization with a mission to guide people to good health through heritage.

ONLINE SHOPPING

American Grass-Fed Beef
americangrassfedbeef.com/grass-fed-natural-beef.asp

An online source for pastured animal products that are delivered to your doorstep.

BuyPortugueseFood.com
buyportuguesefood.com

An online market carrying Portuguese ingredients from bacalhau (salt cod) to linguica, chouriço, and piri piri sauce.

Ditalia
ditalia.com

A gourmet online retailer of all things Italian. Ditalia carries fresh and cured meats, oils and vinegars, cheeses, olives, pasta, rice, jarred tomatoes and sauces, canned fish, honey, and more.

Eat Wild
eatwild.com

This is a terrific database for locating nearby farms and farmers' markets that sell pastured animal products.

La Tienda
tienda.com

This online Spanish market carries Spanish specialties including imported cured meats like jamón serrano and chorizo, Spanish cheeses, bomba rice for paella, and Spanish wines. They also carry paella pans and other Spanish cooking essentials.

Local Harvest
localharvest.org

A directory of local farm stands, farmers' markets, and organic farms.

Odysea
odysea.com

Carries Mediterranean ingredients, with an emphasis on products from Greece, including olives, olive oil, spices, honey, and sauces.

Spanish Table
spanishtable.com

The Spanish Table has three retail shops. They carry Spanish (and Portuguese) ingredients including cured meats, jarred fish, dried beans and rice, olives, olive oil, spices, and condiments. They also carry wines from the region as well as cookware and tableware.

Tenderbelly
tenderbelly.com

A great place to buy naturally raised Berkshire pork, including pork belly and baby back ribs, that is shipped to your home.

Tendergrass Farms
grassfedbeef.com

Another good source of pastured animal meat.

US Wellness Meats
www.grasslandbeef.com

Home delivery of pastured and naturally raised animal products, as well as sustainably sourced seafood.

USDA Directory of Local Farmers Markets
ams.usda.gov/local-food-directories
/farmersmarkets

The USDA's directory for finding nearby farmers' markets.

Zamouri Spices
zamourispices.com

This online retailer specializes in Middle Eastern and North African ingredients. They carry ras al hanout, harissa, Moroccan olives, and olive oil, as well as tagines and other cookware.

Recipe Index

Index

About the Authors

Dorothy Calimeris is a food writer and blogger, a frequent contributor to *Diablo Magazine*, and co-author of the bestselling cookbook, *The Anti-Inflammatory Diet and Action Plans*. A recipe developer and culinary instructor who lives in Oakland, California, with her husband and daughter, she spends her days thinking about what she wants to eat next. Learn more at dorothyeats.com.

Constance Jones is a James Beard Award-winning and best-selling cookbook author who has written about Italian, Japanese, and other international cuisines, as well as nutrition, wine, and beer. As a freelance writer and editor, she has worked with clients such as Zagat Survey, *The New York Times*, *National Geographic Traveler*, Fodor's, and Time Life.